S0-CWX-070

Profit Planning
for
Small Business

Profit Planning
for
Small Business

Robert N. Hogsett

VNR **VAN NOSTRAND REINHOLD COMPANY**
NEW YORK   CINCINNATI   ATLANTA   DALLAS   SAN FRANCISCO
LONDON   TORONTO   MELBOURNE

Van Nostrand Reinhold Company Regional Offices:
New York   Cincinnati   Atlanta   Dallas   San Francisco

Van Nostrand Reinhold Company International Offices:
London   Toronto   Melbourne

Copyright © 1981 by Robert N. Hogsett

Library of Congress Catalog Card Number: 80-24346
ISBN: 0-442-24907-1

All rights reserved. No part of this work covered by the copyright hereon may
be reproduced or used in any form or by any means—graphic, electronic, or
mechanical, including photocopying, recording, taping, or information storage
and retrieval systems—without permission of the publisher.

Manufactured in the United States of America

Published by Van Nostrand Reinhold Company
135 West 50th Street, New York, N.Y. 10020

Published simultaneously in Canada by Van Nostrand Reinhold Ltd.

15   14   13   12   11   10   9   8   7   6   5   4   3   2   1

Library of Congress Cataloging in Publication Data

Hogsett, Robert N
  Profit planning for small business.

  Includes index.
  1. Small business—Management.   I. Title.
HD62.7.H63   658.1'55   80-24346
ISBN 0-442-24907-1

To my beloved wife Dorothy, for forty years a rock of supporting and peaceful stability.

Preface

Profit Planning for Small Business is intended as an aid to the person already operating a small business and to the entrepreneur who intends to open one. The present mortality rate for small businesses is awful to contemplate. It represents a serious drag on the nation's economy as well as a waste of valuable resources, both human and material.

Lack of the refined analytical and planning methods used by large business organizations and lack of the knowledge and financial resources needed to acquire and use these methods contribute substantially to the tremendous yearly loss to the economy. At present, no book exists that is geared to the needs of small businesses while presenting the necessary detailed explanation. There are many college textbooks on the various aspects of modern management methods. However, they are oriented toward employment and application in the large corporate environment; they often have little or no applicability to the problems of the person in a small business.

This book was not written out of an intent to become an author. Instead, it evolved from the author's personal experiences in operating a small business and in advising and consulting with many similar businesses. Its genesis really was in a need for written material to use as handouts for a series of seminars that the author presented in India in 1979. Its basis was a series of explanations of management methods that the author had found useful in operating his own business and in advising others.

The seminars held in India were successful. The author thus believed that similar seminars might be useful in the United States. Naturally, the handouts had to be revised to meet the problems of an American audience. Hence, this book.

It is impossible to give proper recognition to the many whose ideas and thoughts have over the years affected and aided in developing the author's experiential base. There are some special people, however, to whom individual acknowledgment must be given. Special thanks must be given to Carl Heyel—mentor, engineer, author, editor, and long-time friend—without whose advice, guidance, and encouragement the author would not have had the courage to attempt publication, and to Alberta Gordon and Gerry Galbo at Van Nostrand Reinhold whose immense patience, kindness, and good will are beyond description. To these and the many other good friends, colleagues, and associates over many years, a sincere thank you.

ROBERT N. HOGSETT

Contents

EXHIBITS

Profit Planning
for
Small Business

1. Introduction

1. THE PLACE OF SMALL BUSINESS

Small business although individually, perhaps insignificant, is in the aggregate truly big business. So-called small business in total employs almost half of the nation's work force, and produces almost half of the Gross National Product. This is indeed no insignificant force, and its health and prosperity forms the economic base for the entire nation.

Although it receives attention and aid from the government through the Small Business Administration in the form of advice, counseling, loan guarantees, and in some cases, actual low-interest loans, the results are far more apparent than real. Often the best intentioned efforts of SBA field personnel have been hampered and made ineffective by higher bureaucracy, and funds have been wasted by turning the efforts toward unsound and unsuccessful but "sociologically desirable" objectives. Nevertheless, the SBA has done some good.

Other private associations exist to aid small business. The National Federation of Independent Business acts as a lobbying organization to foster a legal climate favorable to small business. The International Council of Small Business exists to develop and disseminate knowledge about and for small business. More and more local chambers of commerce are establishing small business councils for the same purpose on a local level.

The real problem is that the so-called small business community is widely dispersed, and is composed of a great number of highly individualistic people, who are just beginning to find ways to unite. Further, there is really no completely distinguishable segment of the national or world economy which can be labeled exclusively "small business." Economic units range in size from the one-man show to the international giants in a continuous spectrum. No definition has been stated in

1

quantitative terms which will adequately set small business apart from the remainder of the economic community. All big businesses were small at some time in the past. And any small business may bear the seeds of greatness.

The very number and wide dispersal of small business units is of itself a valuable national asset, for it tends to produce a basic stability in the nation's economy. One small business prospers, one declines. One fails today, another springs up tomorrow, and the nation goes on undisturbed by the tragedy. Contrast this with the trauma of a Pennsylvania Railroad bankruptcy, or the tremendous debate over the possible demise of the Chrysler Corporation, and the shock waves which would come from it.

Yet, this basic foundation of our economy suffers the highest mortality rate of any segment. Many of its members lack the knowledge of modern management methods and techniques which give the larger operator a distinct economic edge.

Traditionally, universities have trained for entrance into the larger company, and many medium to large companies contribute heavily to their neighboring universities in order to assure themselves of an adequate reservoir of talent.

However in recent years, perhaps better late than never, many university schools of business and management are directing specific attention to the small business area, to train students to conduct a small business in a sound manner, and to develop improvements in knowledge, techniques, and systems for small business operation. Although this is but a recent development, it bodes well for the future.

Tradition falls hard, and many universities are unable to extend their efforts in this direction because of the lack of finances and financial support. Whether or not this will change in the near future is doubtful, even though the need is being more and more broadly recognized.

With today's ever increasing complications, the owner of a small business faces the problem of constantly improving his knowledge of business operation techniques. Today, the owner or manager of a small business must often truly be broader and more knowledgeable and capable in many more areas than his counterpart in a large company, simply because he cannot afford to hire the specialists; yet he has all the same problems, only differing in the size of the numbers involved.

2. THE PURPOSE OF THIS BOOK

This book is an effort by one man in small business to assist in filling the need for understanding and use of the more sophisticated management techniques in the small business arena. (And it is truly a gladiatorial arena, even though only in an economic sense.) It is not the purpose here to make any new contributions to the general body of management knowledge, but instead to restate proven principles and methods of application in a form, which, it is hoped, will become useful to those who previously have not applied these methods for fine-tuning the finances of small business operation.

If used with patience and understanding, these techniques can do much to restore the traditional soundness and profitability that is inherent in small business, and restore to it the reasonable margin for error which has become eroded to insignificance.

A person would always like to feel that he had something of a fighting chance to succeed. Today, many people in small business feel overwhelmed by the mass of complications in their business environment that they were never trained to deal with.

By many, a person in small business, or even any business, regardless of size, is automatically perceived as rich, conniving, untrustworthy, and an enemy of the common people. With this perception, coupled with the constantly increasing complexity of the economy, technology, and the wilderness of governmental regulations, the person in small business is under pressure to an extent never previously seen. The margin for error has become so small, and the odds against so large, that the slightest error in judgment or planning can become immediately fatal to the enterprise.

Larger businesses, with greater aggregations of capital, can afford to hire specialists to deal with these new problems. Lacking such a depth of resources, the person in small business must do it himself.

Today, that means that he must broaden his knowledge daily, and, to survive, must learn many of the techniques of the larger business and of its different specialists so that he may use them himself. This can be an almost superhuman task, for many of the methods and techniques now in use in the field of modern management have been developed in universities and colleges, and are taught to advanced students at a level far higher than many in small business have had the opportunity to reach.

This can be disheartening. One could well ask whether or not small business is truly doomed; whether anyone can ever catch up, or whether that task has grown beyond human ability. By going back to school, and by burning a lot of midnight oil, the author has managed to acquire knowledge and practice in these techniques, and has found them to be his salvation in running his own business.

Unfortunately, many of these techniques are based on mathematics, and for successful use, require a basic comfort with and knowledge of the essentials of the science. In other words, there is quite a bit of number crunching. This may cause some fear and trembling as the reader sees some of the equations he will be expected to understand and use.

But **BE YE NOT AFRAID,** for it really isn't all that difficult. It is just a somewhat different way of thinking.

The author has been aided by making use of the concept that **mathematics is a special kind of language, with its own rules of grammar and punctuation and no room for words with double meanings, with which to express quantities and relationships precisely.**

It does not substitute for clear thought, but is a tremendous aid because of its precision. So, we shall have to speak a bit of algebra here and there as we go along.

Do not expect to find many final answers in this book. What you will find is what others have found out; ways for **YOU** to seek and find workable answers to the special problems of **YOUR** business.

Our attempt here has been improve the reader's own personal mental tool kit for dealing with his business problems, and coping with the ever more complex business environment in which any business person must operate today.

In the immediately following chapters, we will attempt to lay a foundation of philosophy which, it is hoped, will clarify and identify what the real purpose of business should be. We hope it will also aid the reader to identify for himself the real reasons for taking the great plunge into the business whirlpool. Take time to consider the reasoning displayed as it affects your business and your life.

3. WHAT IS WEALTH?

Wealth is a man-made concept which has been a source of trouble and disagreement since man has been on the earth. People differ on its meaning, sometimes to the extent of bitter and bloody war. Nonetheless, we can all agree that almost all business is really dealing with the creation of wealth, the transfer of wealth, or some combination of the two. Consequently, we should attempt to reach some community of understanding as to its real meaning and importance.

How can we define wealth? Is it the simple knowledge that if we live until tomorrow, we shall at least be able to eat? Is it the possession and control of vast sums of money? Is it the power to compel others to meet our demands? Perhaps it is all of these things and even more, to some people. In most cases, an item of wealth is some physical thing which is generally considered to have value. In other cases, it is the rendering of some kind of service, which is seen to be of value by the one being served.

Here, we immediately beg the question of how value may be defined. We could say simply that value is whatever someone wants, and for which he is willing to exchange something else, including his labor. How great is value? As has been said, it exists in the buyer's mind; and is measured by the depth of desire on the part of the buyer and by how much of what he values he is willing to give up in exchange. In many cases, however, wealth is really material things; a house, land, clothes, good food, work animals, and the like.

One may wonder why money has not been mentioned. There is a good reason. The concept of wealth existed long before money was created, and in a sense, money was invented as a commonly acceptable basis for resolving or compromising differences in value concepts between traders long after trade and business began.

Real wealth, essentially, is physical in nature, and it is wealth only because it is perceived to have value in the mind of a person, although not always of all of mankind. In the main, the desirability of wealth arises not out of its existence, but out of its utility value. Wealth is real wealth because it has utility to man. When the ingredient of real or, at least potential utility is absent, as in the case of false value concepts, what we sometimes call wealth is without real value, and is truly sterile.

We can see the truth of this statement all over the world today because we have come to perceive possession of money as possession of real wealth, while in the meantime the inefficiencies and deliberate deficit spending of governments have eroded and undermined the real value of money everywhere.

If this set of definitions can be accepted, we can look at wealth as something physical or of a service nature, man-made, and deriving its importance from its utility value to man.

In this light, the beginnings of wealth exist in natural resources and in man himself. Natural resources, in and of themselves, are without value, until man finds a use for them. They pre-existed man from the beginning of time. Then how do they become wealth? The atoms did not change, but their form, arrangement, or location was changed.

By the use of man's mind, and muscle, resources are moved and changed in form into something which has utility value to mankind. Iron ore becomes steel. Stone becomes houses. Trees become boats and furniture. The wild grasses become cereal grains for the sustenance of millions.

This indeed is true wealth. And it comes about only through the efforts of man and mankind. If man should disappear, what then would be wealth? Would there be any, lacking mankind or some other intelligent species?

Perhaps (if the reader agrees with Darwin) the monkeys should start over. But so long as man exists in his present form and state of mind, some concept of real wealth such as this will continue, and with it will be business, involving exchange of wealth in some form or other, regardless of the kind or amount of currency in vogue.

Although we will be working with the dollar as currency throughout this book, please keep in mind that it is not the dollar itself that is important; it is the real wealth which that dollar represents that should properly concern us. We should realize that the dollar is only a convenience for denominating and dealing with real wealth.

4. WHY PROFIT?

In these days of Keynesian economics and galloping socialism, the concept of the need for a profit has come into disrepute in "liberal" circles. It is seen by them as an evidence of greed and lack of consideration for humanity on the part of business. Those who seek it are seen by the socialists as leeches, sucking the life blood from the common people. To support a view in opposition is indeed dangerous in some places these days. Nevertheless an opposing view should be advanced, and perhaps vehemently.

Without question there have been and probably still are cases of greedy behavior on the part of some business people who take a greater profit than might be needful. It is suggested, however, that the real issue is how much profit is too much, not whether profits should or should not be made.

One then could well question whether or not this is good. For the "benefit of all the people" should not individuals be restrained from "the exercise of personal greed?" Perhaps, but in practice, it simply doesn't work with human beings as they exist.

The following definition of profit is proposed. It may be considered controversial, but its use may clarify the issues.

> *PROFIT is the creation of wealth in excess of that needed for mere survival.*

If this definition of profit can be accepted, a good case can be made that the existence of profits is essential to the continuance of civilization.

To early man, profit meant, perhaps, working a little extra today to gather fruit for tomorrow's food. Or working late by the fire to chip another spearpoint for hunting, in case his only one broke. Or, perhaps, saving the skin from a kill, so that he could stay warm within it. In any case, these were efforts above the survival level. They go beyond just surviving today, and look toward to providing, not just for tomorrow, but for all the other tomorrows to come.

To put it another way, profits can be equated with savings. And were it not for savings it can be doubted whether civilization would have ever developed.

If one thinks about this matter for a time, he soon comes to realize that without profit, and consequent savings of one sort or another, there would be no reserve of capital and no financial base from which new investments could be made. There would be no reserve for maintenance and repairs. There would be no reserve with which to replace aging or obsolete equipment. There would be nothing with which to pay for research and development. And soon civilization as we know it would grind to a whimpering halt.

To examine this premise further, let us look at the economy of the countries which deny and decry the profit motive. Of these, Soviet Russia is by far the most prominent. If the foregoing premise is true, one can well ask how these people can attain their relatively high standard of living and still deny profits and capitalism.

The answer is that in Russia, capitalism does exist, and profits do exist. The difference is that the profit made is seized by the state instead of accruing to the individual or group which created it. Yet the Russians have not even succeeded in making this work effectively, and have had to turn a blind eye toward individual entrepreneurs and the black market to even have fresh vegetables on the table in season in Moscow. And they have been forced to offer individual rewards and various forms of personal recognition and profit in order to obtain some reasonable level of productivity.

It would seem to be far more effective to make use of the universal human desire for comfort, personal gain, and economic security by promoting the idea of reasonable profits to the individual, rather than attempting to deny the profit principle, and, to effect that denial, to attempt to remake humanity. Those who would seek to eliminate profits would likely be of more true benefit to us all if their attention were to be devoted to the discovery of what should be a reasonable level and rate of individual profit. The element of excessive greed might be eliminated thereby. However, even this wish is not likely to be fulfilled in the near future.

Indeed, without belaboring the point excessively, we can state affirmatively that profits and the profit motive are essential ingredients to the continuation of our civilization. Admitting this fact, and respecting human nature as it really exists, it seems quite unlikely that any group of zealots, no matter how vigorously they puruse their goal, will successfully change human nature in the reasonably near future.

Therefore, as realists, we should then place our attention on securing reasonable profits with greater certainty. Thereby we can be assured of maintaining a sound base for continued development of our civilization. Profits are essential, and if we must disagree about something, let us disagree on how much profit is reasonable.

2. Goals, Objectives, Plans, and the Manager

1. THE PAST, THE PRESENT, AND THE FUTURE

We humans exist in a perpetual instant of "now." Yesterday is gone, never to return. Tomorrow has not yet come, and we cannot see what it will bring. Second by second, minute by minute, our instant of "now" passes along the stream of time, and what is past is gone beyond recovery, forever fixed. We can neither get it back nor change it.

As to the future, we do not know. Yet, despite our own human mortality, we feel compelled to attempt to divine the future; to shape it to our personal ends and purposes, if not for ourselves, then for others. As parents, we do this for our children. As businessmen, we do this for the benefit of ourselves, and for the enterprise. Realizing our own mortality, we seek immortality for our works and enterprises so that they may live after us.

Perhaps this is sheer arrogance on our part. Indeed, there are some who truly think that we should not be concerned with the future. Philosophers may debate its values, politicians may exhort the people to rise against it, and priests may condemn its attention to profit. A philosopher may ask "But why worry about tomorrow? It isn't here, and we may never see it become today."

Businessmen know differently. We answer, "This is the only way we have with which to prepare as best we can for tomorrow's problems, whatever they may be. We may not see it, but chances are very high that someone we care about will see it. And, because we care, we must act as though it will come, and do our best to provide accordingly." Being realists, we are compelled to attempt to maintain continuity.

Somehow, so long as there are people, business and trade must go

Exhibit 1

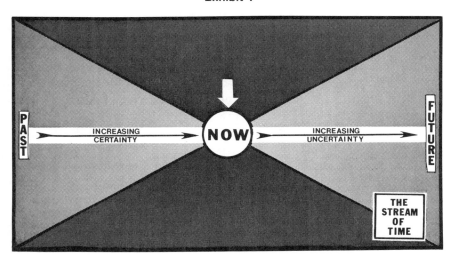

on. We, as business people must provide for the future as best we may regardless of the momentary popularity or unpopularity of our mission. In truth, much of civilization depends upon us.

How then shall we accomplish this task? What are the keys which might unlock the future to our view? We do not have a crystal ball in which we may see the future. We have learned long since that the soothsayer who claims to foretell the future from the intestines of slain animals or birds is a fraud, even though there are some who still believe in such things. Experience has proved these methods to be incapable of making really sound and reliable predictions. So, then, what shall we do? We, as businessmen, are driven to attempt to view the future, yet we cannot. How, then, shall we attempt to solve this dilemma?

We must remember the past, and learn from it. We can then assume that what happened once may happen again, and if a pattern has been repeated, it is likely to continue to be repeated. We have mentioned experience frequently, and sages have told us that it is indeed the best teacher.

We have agreed that we must plan and think for the future if we are to be good businessmen. We have established that past history and our ability to reason are all the resources we have from which to fashion a springboard into the future. In primitive tribes, history is handed down from one generation to another by verbal repetition and memorization.

Yet our memories are fragile and undependable; hardly a basis from which to operate a complex business.

This means only one thing. Since we cannot trust memory, we must develop other means to capture and retain the vital happenings of each day, month, or year. This means that this information must be preserved in some much more permanent medium. We must have good records. They must be accurate, both as to time, and as to event information. And, if they are to have their maximum value, they must be up to date.

Since these records of the business history become the basis for the formulation of management plans and programs, they must be in management's hand promptly. Failure to have up-to-date information as a basis for decisions has caused the premature death of more than one enterprise throughout the world.

Newton stated that until you have measured something, you are ignorant about it, but once you have measured it, you have indeed learned something useful about it. Businessmen are forever asking "how much?" If history is to be truly useful, it must not only answer what happened, and when, but how much. Records must be quantitative.

It has been generally agreed that basing decisions on obsolete information can be more damaging to the enterprise than having no information at all and making decisions by the flip of a coin. At least, then, one has a 50% chance of being right.

But, you may ask, what is this so essential information? Primarily it is the information furnished by the two main types of accounting reports; the Balance Sheet, and the Income Statement. It is numbers, and it is measurements. It is records.

The maintenance of up-to-date, comprehensive records is often viewed as a major burden by many people in smaller businesses. They tend to think of this burden as "Something I have to do for the *-*- government," or for "The *-*-*-*- banker." Nothing could be further from the truth.

While it is certainly true that preparation of these reports, and maintenance of the required records in an up-to-date condition requires effort, and this effort must be taken from the total effort available to run the enterprise, these records and reports should not be considered to be an unnecessary burden. They are really a matter of the greatest importance to the manager. Only in this way can an adequate, accurate, quantitative decision base be supplied to the manager for his use in making the business prosper.

Our theme of Profit Planning, planning to make business profitable and keeping it that way, will be served in detail later on by discussions of the various ways management science has given us to make use of this quantitative decision base. At the moment, let it suffice to say that to serve as a decision base for good management, accounting records must be maintained with accuracy, promptness, and in sufficient detail to yield definitive answers where possible.

The question then comes to mind, "How much detail should I have in my accounting records?" The answer is not an easy one. Lacking a computer, one is confronted with the cost of creating detail in records, which can be not only expensive in labor cost, but time-consuming, often delaying prompt report preparation, and thus defeating its purpose. Great strides are now being made in the United States in the use of "microcomputers" for the preparation of accounting reports, as well as various other reports on operations.

With the availability of some types of computer, and with adequate programming support, the danger is of another type; that of attempting so much detail that no one ever really looks at the reports, and important facts become drowned in the mass of information.

This type of behavior is somewhat typical of the aggressive but short-sighted manager who aspires to do a superior job. With the onset of computer capability, he becomes enthralled with the possible amount of detail he can receive which he never could before, and simply goes overboard, very soon finding himself drowning in sea of computer print-outs. Often too, such a person, uninformed of the limitations of computers, enters with the idea that acquisition of a computer will act with some type of mysterious magic to cure all his problems.

Computers, indeed, can act very quickly, and are capable of producing vast amounts of data in a very short time. However, they are also very stupid but compliant servants who will obey one's slightest wish, but only in their own fashion. They will do precisely and only that which you instruct them to do. Consequently, if the system is not properly designed, it will fail, or produce wrong results, sometimes to the point of absolute absurdity.

It is of vital importance when changing systems, or when contemplating computerization, that the revisions be clearly established and that the system be operating effectively on a manual basis before installing the computer. When that has been accomplished, the computer then can take over the work and do it very quickly. Failing to assure the existence of this situation, however, almost certainly jeopardizes the value of any investment in computerization.

2. GOALS AND OBJECTIVES

A traveler usually has a destination or goal in mind. Without it, he becomes only an aimless wanderer buffeted by the winds of adverse fate, and surviving only by chance instead of by design.

So it is with business. Without a goal, a purpose for being, a "base course" cannot be established. The enterprise can only drift aimlessly with the winds, abandoned to whatever circumstances may occur. We have set out that the making of reasonable profit should be the goal of a business. "But is that all?" one may ask. The answer is "No." There is much more. The owner's personality, his abilities, his aspirations, the environment in which he operates, the state of the economy, and a myriad of other factors affect such a basic decision. The setting of goals for a business is indeed a serious matter, not to be taken lightly.

Such a goal may be impossible of achievement, as with the goal of the industrial engineer, whose eternal aspiration is to create the perfect job. This goal, forever pursued, is the creation of a job of useful work, creating wealth, but which, in the creation, would require expenditure of neither labor, energy, nor time.

Obviously, this is a goal impossible of achievement. However, by persevering along the path toward that impossible goal, the engineer does manage to make progress in minimizing waste and in increasing prudent and effective use of that most precious resource, man's effort.

The principal problem in setting goals for any business is that of defining the goal. This must be done in such a manner as to be clearly understood by all those who might be involved in attempting to attain it. It should be precise, yet general. It is not enough to say "Our goal is to make money," or "My goal is to become a rich person." How much money is enough? What is "rich?"

We should try to think of goals in more definite terms, such as "Our goal is to become debt free by the end of 1984," or "I wish to create an estate of one hundred thousand dollars for my wife, and a similar amount for each of my children within the next twenty years." In other words, goals should be stated as precisely and clearly as possible, and preferably with some type of time schedule for attainment.

Again, either the goal, or the time schedule, or both, may be unattainable in fact, yet still be worthy of pursuit. And the test of worthiness should be applied. Such a test is not easily done, and often involves the sense of values of the owner or manager. To the extent that these values are practical and reasonable, goals based on them are likely to be effective. Lacking such realism of value judgment, goals are likely to become amorphous, ineffective, and, consequently without real value.

Having a goal or final destination is not enough. Almost always, no matter how well stated, goals are broad, and the path or paths toward achieving them are often not clear. An intermediate step is needed to make their implementation practical and effective.

This we can call setting up objectives, or way-stations en route to the final destination. Several orders of importance of these objectives are possible, and often occur, even as a traveler may take several stages during a day, resting at each, before reaching his evening's resting place, and having done so, not yet has reached his final destination.

The important thing about objectives is that they be stated in sufficient detail and set within a sufficiently short time span that their attainment is seen as reasonable and possible; that they are essentially "do-able" tasks, and are generally recognized as such.

This is a technique of management now under wide discussion and adoption labeled "Management by Objectives" which actually involves doing these precise things, and setting a timetable for their accomplishment. Management then is evaluated by its progress toward attainment of the objectives within the prescribed time frame.

Establishment of a goal and a hierarchy of intermediate objectives, while worthy things to do, are not sufficient to attain good operation. Yet another ingredient is needed.

As conditions change in the business environment, values may also

Exhibit 2

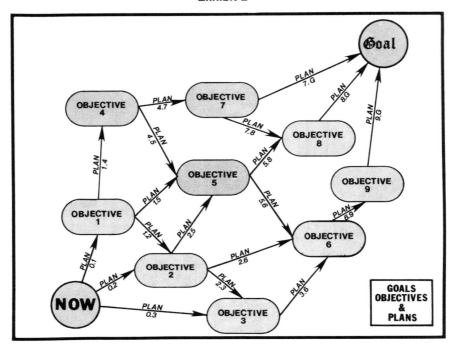

change, and goals and objectives may be invalidated as a result. To survive and prosper, a business must move with those changes.

3. PLANS AND THE GAME OF "WHAT IF?"

There is often more than one path toward an objective, and often more than one objective on the way toward a company goal. Selection of the correct path under changing circumstances is one of management's most important chores. Such selection demands exploration and evaluation of all the possible paths and objectives. Means for improving selection among alternatives and decision making are discussed in Chapter 11, Section 3.

Shifting circumstances in business, often arising from outside the business, such as changes in economic climate, competition, regulations, and many others of a similar nature require an almost constant reservoir of new or changed plans. And not all plans are of equal value or feasibility. Similarly, objectives may require review and modification or change.

Development of the various alternatives is often a demanding exercise of the imaginative powers, as well as of the understanding of the environment in which the business must function. Management must constantly play the game of "What If   ?", erecting possible contingent events which could influence progress toward a particular objective, and developing alternative tactics and strategy, including changes in objectives as necessary.

All of us do or should do a similar type of thinking when driving on the highway. What if the person ahead suddenly changes lanes? What if the car coming down the side road does not stop? What if that boy hits a stone and falls off his bicycle? What will you do? We call this "Defensive Driving." A good manager must also drive his business defensively.

A good way of attacking this ongoing problem is through the technique of brainstorming. Three steps are involved, which usually need to be taken one at a time, separately, and in order.

1. **CLARIFYING AND STATING THE PROBLEM**
2. **IDEA GENERATION**
3. **EVALUATION**

As is often the case, once one has defined and stated the problem correctly, the solution is half-way gained. To benefit fully from brainstorming, as from any other mode of problem-solving, correctly identifying, defining, and stating the problem is vital.

The Idea Generation step is most important. It should be conducted under the following rules.

1. **ANY IDEA IS ACCEPTABLE,** no matter how unusual.
2. **NO CRITICISM OR EVALUATION IS PERMITTED** during the idea generation stage.
3. **ALL IDEAS ARE REDUCED TO WRITING.**

At another session, the third step, that of Evaluation is undertaken. Steps two and three should be somewhat separated in time so as to permit participants to begin some private evaluation and preparation of support or criticism of the various ideas previously generated.

Not all plans are equally feasible or desirable. Consequently, some means of comparison and evaluation, preferably of a quantitative nature, are required. Most often, this takes the form of some type of cost-to-benefit analysis. Again, reference to Chapter 11, Section 3 is recommended.

The most important point in this stage is the attempt at **OBJECTIVE** evaluation of **ALL** alternatives. Although differences of opinion will develop, they should enlighten but should not generate unproductive heat. The following rules should apply.

1. **NO IDEA IS EVER RIDICULOUS.**
2. **NO PERSONAL RIDICULE OR ATTACK MAY BE PERMITTED.**
3. **CRITICISM SHOULD BE BASED ON QUANTITATIVE FACT WHENEVER POSSIBLE, AND ON OBJECTIVE JUDGMENT OTHERWISE.**

Particular care needs to be taken at this step. Being human and egotistic to a greater or lesser degree, we often tend to fall in love with our own ideas, sometimes to the extent of developing a serious case of "tunnel vision" toward alternatives or ideas which we did not generate. This often leads to lack of objectivity, undue defensiveness, and attack or ridicule on a personal basis. This cannot be tolerated lest the entire benefit of the technique be lost.

We can summarize by stating again that we must have goals. We must break them down into subsidiary, attainable objectives, and we must formulate plans for their attainment, weighing the costs and benefits of each alternative in order to select and implement the correct plan.

In so doing, we must remember that this is a job which is never completed. It is and must be an ongoing process of continuing modification, adjustment, and idea generation to meet the ever-changing environment in which we must operate.

Contingency planning, playing the game of "What If?" is more than a game. It is one of the most important things a management can do to maintain a sound business.

As we will see in later chapters, much of Management Science today is oriented toward supplying more accurate quantitative estimates and statements of probabilities, and encouraging a greater degree of objectivity in the making of plans and decisions by management. Great strides in this direction have been made in the second half of the twentieth century.

4. SYSTEM AND CONTROL

We have seen the need to look to the past as a guide to the future. We have also seen that the past is not a certain and sure guide, and that as we attempt to reach further into the future, we encounter increasing uncertainty in general, and more than anything, increasing *certainty* that some change will happen. Consequently, managers have always been concerned with attempting to forecast the future, with which we will deal in more detail in a later chapter, and with controlling and making the necessary changes in the conduct of the business to meet the changing environment in which the business must operate.

Today's manager, more than ever before, is concerned with controlling his business and instituting appropriate changes in its mode and condition of operation in order to attain the desired level of profit. We shall not attempt to state at this point what that desired level might be, but we can be assured that there will be one for any business, manager, or operator.

In today's economy, business is neither simple, nor isolated. The environment in which the smaller business must operate contains a constantly diminishing margin for error in decision making. And more than ever, any business is a totality of often conflicting elements which interact in a complex fashion. In many cases, the level of complexity develops to a level beyond the capacity of the owner-manager's grasp. Such a situation often begets immediate difficulty, and has contributed substantially to the current high mortality rate in the small business sector.

Business must be considered as a set of interacting systems, not operating alone, but in an environment of change which impacts continually upon conduct of the enterprise. Today, governmental regulations and requirements make a truly formidable impact on business operations throughout the world, in addition to hurricanes, droughts, floods, and other natural and human-induced circumstances.

In many cases, the raw material of one business is the finished product of another. Under today's circumstances, it is not enough merely to buy what the market offers, at its price; it becomes necessary to shop, to establish specifications, and means for comparing different offerings in the marketplace. An organized system is needed to accomplish these things. And such a system must be designed and planned to operate effectively so that the business continues profitable operation without interruption.

The processing internal to the enterprise is another set of subsystems, requiring design, control and supervision, even though the enterprise be only displaying and selling the products of others without change.

As a part of management science, as well as of several of the other new branches of science which have developed in recent years, has been the study of systems and of their design and operation, and determination of how control is really exercised. Statement of the principles and mode of operation of feedback looping as a control means is one development in the general area of Management Science.

Feedback Looping is simply starting with a planned or desired path or series of actions, sensing or detecting deviations from the planned path or actions, making a judgment as to the direction and extent of the deviation, taking appropriate corrective action (instituting change), and resensing the result, as seen in the following diagram.

Operation under feedback control principles demands that there be a "base course" or some sort of statement of desired behavior, stated in the form of some types of Goals, Objectives, and Plans. These must be established by management from analysis of its needs and plans, as will be discussed in greater depth in later sections. Without a "base course," there is no "starting point" or baseline from which to sense deviations, and, therefore, control becomes impossible.

Then there must be means for detecting the direction, amount, and

Exhibit 3

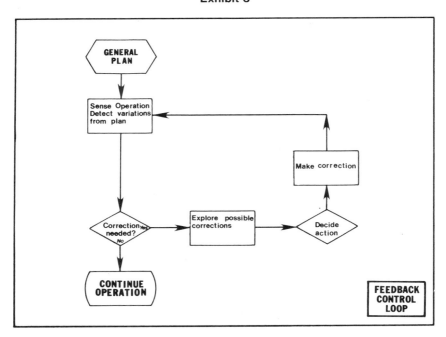

rate of change as it occurs. The typical manager is, among other things, a sensing and judgment-making agent as to when, how, and how much correction to introduce. Second, there must be a means of measuring deviations. Lacking measurement of these factors, our attempts to control would be futile, since we would have no way of determining how much correction to apply.

Fulfillment of these two primary requirement does not guarantee the existence of effective control. Another key factor is the speed with which the feedback control loop can operate. At minimum, the loop must operate with sufficient speed to initiate the proper degree of corrective action to catch the out-of path situation before it becomes uncorrectable.

It is sometimes the case that the power to instigate corrective action is limited by physical, legal, moral, or other constraints. Unless the feedback loop can operate effectively within the time and power limits imposed by these constraints, out-of-control situations become possible. An example from life is that of a motorist who has a tire blowout at high speed. *Unless his feedback loop operates very quickly, and he has the physical power to overcome the drag of the blown tire, he may be killed.*

Many business and economic phenomena operate in a cyclical pattern, in which direction will reverse at intervals. It is a known fact that if the operation of the feedback control loop is too slow relative to the natural cycle, or if the applied correction is not proportional to the extent of deviation, a push becomes, in fact, a pull, and, instead of dampening out oscillations from the desired "base course," oscillations are increased, sometimes to the point of destruction of the system.

Physical examples of this phenomenon can be seen in the novice auto driver or airplane pilot, who, at the beginning, is rarely able to maintain a steady course. Disturbances originating from exterior sources upset the direction, and the driver does not react quickly enough nor judge correctly the amount of correction to apply. The result is a weaving path, which can go out of control completely.

Therefore, control loops must be assured of operating with sufficient speed, accuracy, and proportionality of power application to damp out variability instead of enhancing it. Developing such assurance within the system is another of management's major responsibilities.

So far, then, we have developed the need for control, the use of the feedback principle as a means of control, the responsibility we feel to look toward the future, and the fact that we, as businessmen, are inclined toward dealing with some kinds of numbers and feel the definite need to do so.

It must be remembered that the obligation of the manager to exercise control, and to use feedback control principles effectively is not a one-time thing. It is an on-going responsibility. As the effectiveness of control increases, so does the demand for increased precision in sensing and application of proportional corection.

We can then investigate what techniques are available from the reservoirs of management science and procedure with which to fill these needs.

5. THE MANAGER: AN AGENT FOR CHANGE

Operation and control of a business is conducted in an ever-present atmosphere of change. Today is never exactly like yesterday, and the course of the busines is always in need of adjustment. Remember that change is **FUTURE ORIENTED.**

Much of a manger's time during the day is spent "putting out fires" caused by variations from plan, accidents, and changes in environment. This is particularly so in the small business environment on which local conditions bear much greater influence. This fireman act often intrudes severely on the ability to plan and to play the game of "What If?"

This becomes a situation of mere reaction, of almost the "knee-jerk" variety, in which the manager is thrown about and controlled by events instead of controlling them. From this abyss of reaction, the manager will never emerge unless he takes some positive steps. Substantial advances and improvements are unlikely without specific management action. The manager must initiate changes and improvements, and encourage their development and proposal by his subordinates.

In so doing, there is an attitude which should be cultivated, for it will lead to ever-increasing benefits. Complacency in a business can be fatal. A business may be very good, but its competitors can be also. It may have the best product, but not forever. If any business remains complacent, it will soon be passed by. Until perfection is reached, improvement is always possible, and someone sooner or later will make that improvement; if not you, it will be your competitor.

The necessary attitude is one of **CONSTRUCTIVE DISSATISFACTION.** It arises from a realization that to be complacent is to court disaster, that improvement is possible, and that continuing improvement is essential to good health for the business. To be constructive, dissatisfaction with things as they are should be rational, not emotional. It should never result in nagging and complaining to subordinates or others.

A pattern of nagging or antagonistic behavior by management is likely to induce active opposition before too long. Constructive dissatisfaction can better be expressed in the form of praise for accomplishment of improvements and encouragement toward continued improvement in all aspects of the business.

To do this requires that the mind of the manager must remain flexible. He must be awake to the possibilities for change and improvement, even more than being acutely sensitive to environmental changes and reacting to them promptly. He must seek out improvements, taking an active, seeking role, rather than a passive or reactive one. To be successful, he must truly be an agent for change.

Playing the game of "What If" has other implications. Setting up various scenarios of possibility also implies the need to make choices and selections; in other words, making decisions. Indeed, much of management is "Decisions, Decisions!" Consequently, the process of decision making has come under study in recent years. Some techniques have emerged from the laboratory which have proved quite useful to operating managers.

One of our principal thrusts in modern management has been to get measured facts as a substitute for guesses and hunches whenever possible; to attempt to reduce the diameter of the circle of uncertainty which surrounds every decision. To this point, we have not dealt with how to do this.

An organized method of approach has been developed, using two major considerations. First is the determination of all of the various alternatives. Here, the brainstorming technique mentioned previously will be of great help. Second, is the determination of payoff amounts for each sequence of events. Of course, the payoff for some of the alternatives could be a loss of some type.

Naturally, one normally seeks to maximize profits and minimize or eliminate losses. Complete elimination of the potential for loss is almost impossible. There can always be times when we simply must accept some loss, albeit grudgingly, and simply do all we can to minimize its bad effects.

However, it is early in our exposition, and you, the reader, have not yet reached the sections in which we begin to deal with the mathematical methods of determining payoff amounts, and making decisions "in the modern manner." We will do so in later sections of this book, after you have had an opportunity to do a little "number crunching" to get into practice.

The thing to remember, at this point of progress, and as we go further along, is that we want to go about the making of decisions and plans in an organized, systematic manner, using objective information and measured facts as much as possible, leaving out emotion, and making subjective estimates only in cases where they are better than no estimate at all. This, together with maintaining faithfully the mental orientation of **CONSTRUCTIVE DISSATISFACTION** will do much to help anyone to become a better and more innovative manager of his affairs.

3. Setting Profit Targets

1. CONSIDERATIONS

In attempting to establish a profit target, some rough rules may be advanced, based upon the intuitively sound concept of the availability of free choice on the part of an investor, and the existence of a free market, competing for profitable investments and for capital. Although these freedoms may not always completely exist in practice, their use affords a logical basis for targeting a profit.

In a free society, the investor has free choice as to what he does with his money. As we live in a free society, we must recognize that he has options and choices open to him as to his investment. As managers, we must recognize this situation as reality. We must therefore supply him with an adequate reason to choose favorably for our enterprise.

Most investors invest for the purposes of gaining income, increasing capital wealth, or a mixture of both. More often than not, the investor's interest is on the income to be received. This means essentially that a manager or owner must be aware of the state of the investment market and of the range of choices open to a potential or existing investor.

The typical investor, as opposed to a sophisticated one, is interested principally in the income he receives from his investment. This usually is taken to mean return on equity, or return on the ownership portion of the business. In present-day situations, this consideration is inadequate.

It is a generally accepted axiom that risk and reward should go hand-in-hand; that the greater the risk, the greater the reward potential, and vice versa. Thus, in an investment sense, as might be expected, the investments with the lowest level of perceived risk and greatest measure of security traditionally have the lowest yields.

Perceptions of risk will vary from one investor to another, and may not even be realistic in fact. Nevertheless, these perceptions must be dealt with as though they were fact, for it is upon these perceptions that the investor will make his decision.

It is a known fact that whatever a person perceives or believes to be true is indeed true to that person, regardless of facts, opinions, or beliefs held by others. It will not change unless the person himself changes his perception or belief.

Perceptions are influenced by the quantity and quality of the past history or "track record" of the enterprise. If there is little or no track record, investment judgments and decisions are apt to be made on subjective or emotional grounds, and often with higher perceptions of risk than need be. This presents a particularly difficult situation to the developer of a new and unfledged business, or the smaller business with only a limited track record.

It is well known that the less one needs money, the easier it is to obtain, and sarcastic comments to this effect are often made by those starting a new business, or those whose businesses may be in need of added capital but are not in a strong position. Although it is of little help to such a person, the logical position of the investor and the banker needs some understanding to place things in perspective.

As a result, the perceived level of risk is a potent consideration affecting the investor's choice among competing investments. Consequently, we should be governed by the following rules.

1. **THE INVESTMENT MUST OFFER A COMPETITIVE AND ATTRACTIVE RETURN AGAINST ALL OTHERS WITH THE SAME PERCEIVED LEVEL OF RISK.**

2. **THE RISK OF SUBSTANTIAL OR PERMANENT LOSS MUST BE PERCEIVED AS BEING RELATIVELY LOW.**

The true capital of a business includes not only the owner's equity, but any borrowed funds in addition. A principle of operation, currently in wide use, holds that if, by using borrowed money, one can obtain a yield or profit in excess of the rental cost of the money borrowed, it is wise to borrow.

This principle, commonly called "leveraging," works well in times of inflation and economic expansion. The effects of inflation are particularly beneficial to use of leveraging, for the borrower repays the borrowed money dollar for dollar with cheaper money which was easier to obtain.

There is a major warning that should be kept in mind in considering use of this strategy. When times are good, and everything is on the upward trend, it becomes very appealing. However, there is always the possibility of a down-turn in the economy. When this occurs, making principal and interest payments on borrowings can easily become a weight sufficiently heavy to sink many a business forever. Caution should always be exercised so as not to become overextended with debt.

Another factor to be kept in mind in using this strategy under today's situation of rapid inflation coupled with rapidly rising interest rates is that of the net benefit after taxes. It affects the choice of borrowing versus expending capital, or the choice of whether or not to pay off previous borrowings prematurely.

Although interest is tax deductible as a cost of doing business, after $100,000 of pretax annual profit, the tax rate is 48%. The pretax dollar paid out in interest only costs the company $.52. Careful comparison must be made both before and after taxes, of net earnings, including the earnings on invested capital surplus and retained earnings, the loss of those earnings by early debt payoff, and the gross and net cost of borrowing.

Since borrowings have the same effect on the company's working capital as investments in equity, the profit target should be so established as to yield the same return on borrowed funds as on equity, or, in other words, on the total funds employed.

The investor makes his investment to earn money; to obtain a profit, and to have reasonable assurance of being able to get back his original investment. Although, indicative of the existence of risk (some losses do occur) no one undertakes real losses of capital willingly, despite the present income-tax situation which appears to some to make losses undesirable. The real fact is that this becomes desirable only under special circumstances, where, due to some peculiarity in tax law, a loss is on paper only, and does not result in a real loss of capital.

This same situation applies to borrowing. Bankers' judgments are based upon their perceptions of risk, although they often go further toward objectivity by searching for facts to support their judgments.

In the case of the banker, money is his inventory, which he rents from investors or users of his services, and lends out in hope of a profit. To stay in business, he must have repayment of his loans in order to have funds with which to make other loans. He is in a continuous state of dilemma. He must take some risk if he is to make a profit (by making loans at interest). At the same time, he dare not have heavy losses, or fail to secure timely repayment very often, for he is usually not working with his own money.

Most of the time he is working with your money and that of other depositors. You would become quite upset if, on going to the bank to cash a check for grocery money, the banker told you that he didn't have any money because he lent it out and it wasn't repaid on time.

The perception of risk is a major consideration in determining both the availability of money, and the rent or rate of return which must be paid for its use. An astute manager must always keep this fact in mind.

Almost everywhere in the world, business is taxed in some way; most usually upon earnings or profits. In establishing a profit target, consideration must always be given to the problem of providing for taxes out of pretax profits, for the yield to owners and investors, at least in the United States, comes after taxes are deducted from the earnings of the enterprise.

There is also the matter of providing for the growth and future financial needs of the enterprise. This is usually done by retaining a certain portion of earnings in the business instead of distributing all to the investors in the form of dividends. Although this truly increases stockholders' wealth, it is not often so perceived by the typical investor. He cannot eat or spend retained earnings unless he sells his stock.

Consequently the prudent manager of a publicly held company will gage his profit target on paying not only a competitive cash dividend, but adding a substantial amount to retained earnings after taxes. A good rule of thumb is to put a dollar into retained earnings for each dollar to be paid in dividends. Owner-managers and those in smaller, privately held enterprises can make good use of this same kind of rule.

In profit planning, for the operating manager, who must think in pretax terms, it is necessary to mark up all post-tax profit targets so as to account for the probable taxes. A suitable formula for doing so follows.

Post-Tax to Pretax Markup

Where:

P = Pretax Profit
P_t = Profit after taxes
T = Probable tax rate, as a decimal

Equation 1:

$$P = \frac{P_t}{1 - T}$$

Strict observation of both of the two following rules should aid in keeping these requirements clearly in mind.

1. PEOPLE WHO WORK SHOULD EARN MONEY

If an owner-manager of a small business cannot earn as much for his actual labor as he could being employed by someone else, something is wrong with his judgment, or he is making his decision to remain in business for other than financial reasons.

2. MONEY WHICH WORKS SHOULD EARN MONEY

If an owner-manager cannot realize a return on the investment in his business at least competitive with what that money would earn if invested elsewhere at the same level of risk, something is also wrong with his judgment or with his perception of the risk of his business.

This need is often ignored or not understood by the owner-managers of small businesses. Often they equate profits from the business with their own earnings for their labor without regard to any return on the investment made to start and sustain the business. The situation is often made more difficult by the frequent tendency of the new entrepreneur to "buy his way into the market" with low prices.

This can be a serious error, for, when growth demands hiring someone else to do some of the work previously done by the owner-manager, there often isn't enough contribution left to provide a living for the owner-manager with his enlarged responsibilities.

It should be noted here that because of necessary self-confidence in his abilities, the entrepreneurial type of person has a lower perception of the risk level of his business than objective outside appraisal would indicate. This complicates his problem of convincing bankers (traditionally pessimists on appraisal and perceptions of risk), and other investors as well, of the soundness of his proposed new venture.

In summation, a profit target would be an appropriate "after tax" return on funds employed (the summation of a competitive return to investors and an appropriate addition to retained earnings) after competitive owner-manager salaries have been paid. This after-tax target should then be marked up by the anticipated tax rate, as given by the preceding formula, to obtain the pretax profit target for operating purposes.

2. EXCESSIVE PROFIT?

The problem of distinguishing an excessive profit from a reasonable one is difficult at the very least, for the definition of excessive profit is highly flexible, and will vary according to who is paying and who is taking the profit. Of course, there are those who would eliminate profit entirely, suggesting and even urging that everyone work for love.

This might be an ideal situation if things never wore out, if we had reached the pinnacle of advancement in all fields, and if we had no further need for replacements or for research and development. These things have not happened, and we have already demonstrated that without the ideal environment, the theory of the idealists simply does not work. The true zealots who would do away with profits should, perhaps, be left to enjoy fully the true fruits of their desires. Perhaps realizing their wishes might awake them to reality.

The fact is that any business, as well as civilization itself, must have profits to survive and provide improving standards of living for humanity. A failure of profits unerringly leads to the eventual demise of the business. One should remember that the only utility value of a corpse is to a cannibal, or to a scavenger (neglecting its minor value as fertilizer), and that the duty of every person in business is to <u>SUR-</u>

VIVE AND BE PROFITABLE, for only thereby can anyone in business create the necessary surplus profit by which the lot of humanity can be made better.

We have agreed that some profit is essential, that business cannot operate without it, and neither can civilization for very long. It might be worthwhile to investigate possible ways of determining what a fair profit might be. In our own national history, we have seen concentrations of economic power develop which exploited their monopolistic positions and profited enormously. So much so that the people rose up and successfully demanded legal action to curtail such power.

The theory on which our economy is run is that of a free market, in which prices are pretty well determined by supply and demand. When overproduction occurs, when production exceeds demand, prices tend to drop as sellers compete for the buyers' scarce dollars. Among other things, this tends to drive inefficient producers out of the market because they cannot meet the competition. Conversely, when a scarcity develops, prices rise as buyers compete with dollars for a limited supply of goods. The idea is that this type of competition will tend to balance and control supply, demand, and price.

In a simple or ideal economy, this works well. In the real world, however, things are more complex, and there have been more and more interferences with the operation of a totally free market. There have been many plausible reasons for such interference. The nation may lack certain resources, and decide to pay a premium in order to maintain that capacity within its control. Special interests, such as labor, oil producers, farmers, and others seek legislation to protect themselves and what they believe to be their financial well-being from the unfavorable effects of full free-market operation.

In recent decades, in the U.S. as well as elsewhere in the world, there has been more and more governmental tinkering with free-market operation for various reasons. While such tinkering does not wholly inhibit free-market operation, it confuses the issues severely.

Free-market operation, which tends to stabilize itself over time, operates much more rapidly than the ponderous operation of the feedback loop of usual governmental remedial actions, with the result that very often, even the best intended governmental action ends by being precisely the wrong thing to have done.

Nonetheless, this pressure to enact legislation exists, and any easily visible attempt at gaining what the general public believes to be excessive profit is likely to receive severe treatment.

For the great bulk of the population who wish to maintain civilization and those in business who wish to provide for the future by making a profit, defining a reasonable profit remains a question.

High prices can be justified to a considerable extent and be willingly accepted by the public, if that public perceives that the product or service being offered is superior to competition. As public perception of quality declines, price resistance increases.

Advertising contributes much to public perception, and can do much to create a favorable image. Such an image must be backed up by reasonable fact, however, for if the perceived image turns out to be false, the backlash can cause severe damage to the company. There is no worse enemy to a business than a customer who feels abused, even though the abuse may not be real.

The best answer which can be given is, perhaps, that of using the criteria in the preceding chapter as a base, or minimum target. Even this may be criticized by nonreasoning people, but if the need for that level of profit is demonstrable, criticism should not be severe. Beyond this level, if, through the existence of a seller's market, market conditions permit an improved profit, it certainly should be taken, but not as a price increase leader.

In this respect, one should refer to the fundamental idea of compromise, as it operates in a nonmonetary bartering situation. Each party to a transaction begins with a set of aspirations or wishes, generally wishing to get as much as possible, while giving as little as possible. Obviously, if each party held rigidly to his initial goal, there would never be a trade.

That trade exists indicates that the parties thereto are less than absolutely rigid in pursuit of their personal goals. Consequently, each retreats to some extent from his initial position, exacting some previously unoffered gain from his opponent in exchange for his own retreat from his previous position; each in turn, until a level is reached at which each party feels he has gained as much as possible for what he has had to give. At that level, an effective compromise has been reached, and a deal is made. Each party, although dissatisfied in not having gained his initial target, generally leaves the transaction with the feeling that he can somehow live with the result.

To the extent that the initial bargaining positions and economic power are unequal, this concept fails in practice, at least partially, for this principle of compromise, and the reaching of "livable" levels as deals are made demands something near equality of bargaining and economic power for both parties to the transaction. The person in small business rarely finds himself in such a position of equality, except, perhaps, in dealing with an individual customer. More often, he is making the best deal he can.

The key, possibly, is in getting all the market will bear, without being unbearable about it. For judging whether or not a profit is excessive is entirely a matter of relativity, and of one's own point of view.

4. Techniques for Examining Business Behavior

1. BALANCE SHEET RATIO ANALYSIS

Almost since the development of double-entry bookkeeping methods, bankers and financial analysts have made use of balance sheets, and of certain ratios between various balance sheet components in order to determine the health of the enterprise. Many business operators, particularly those in the smaller businesses, do not understand the reason for or the meaning of the balance sheet itself, let alone understanding these ratios and their meaning. Consequently they cannot use this vital document or its ratios for their own benefit.

The balance sheet is made up of three principal components, with which many are unfamiliar. These are **ASSETS, LIABILITIES,** and **EQUITY.** We can define these as follows.

Assets

The monetary value of all the PROPERTY which the business owns or has a right to.

Liabilities

The monetary value of RIGHTS to the property of the business owned by others as a result of debts, taxes, court judgments, or other promises.

Equity

The monetary value of the RIGHTS to the property of the business remaining for the owners after LIABILITIES are deducted.

Each of these major components is subdivided into various classifications, and, as we shall see below, comparisons between various of these subdivisions in the form of ratios between them will tell us a great deal about the business.

In making up a balance sheet, the various types of **ASSETS** are normally shown on the left side in the order of decreasing liquidity or ease of convertibility into money, with money itself being first; then accounts receivable, inventory, and other assets. The various types of **LIABILITIES** are shown at the top of the right-hand side in descending order of the immediacy of their requirements for payment; accounts payable first, then short-term loans, then long-term borrowings.

The various components of **EQUITY, Common Stock, Capital Surplus, and Retained Earnings** take the remaining positions on the right side, so that in total:

ASSETS EQUAL LIABILITIES PLUS EQUITY

A brief review of the most commonly used of these ratios will be useful. Below is a typical balance sheet of a manufacturing company from which we will take our examples.

Exhibit 4

BALANCE SHEET

XYZ COMPANY

June 30, 1979

ASSETS		LIABILITIES & EQUITY	
Cash	177,689	Accounts Payable	175,042
Accounts Receivable	678,279	Loans and Notes	448,508
Inventories	1,328,963	Accrued Taxes	36,203
Prepaid Expenses	20,756	Other Liabilities	190,938
Tax Prepayments	35,203		
		Current Liabilities	850,691
Current Assets	2,240,890		
		Long Term Debt	604,168
Fixed Assets, Cost	1,596,886		
Less Depreciation	856,829	TOTAL LIABILITIES	1,454,859
Net Fixed Assets	740,057	EQUITY	
Long Term Investment	65,376	Common Stock	420,828
Goodwill	205,157	Capital Surplus	361,158
		Retained Earnings	1,014,635
		TOTAL EQUITY	1,796,621
TOTAL ASSETS	3,251,480	TOTAL LIAB. & EQUITY	3,251,480

As we can see, a BALANCE SHEET is a numerical picture of the status of the enterprise at a particular instant in time. As such, it has meaning and usefulness, even though it is essentially static. You will note that the total ASSETS, appearing on the left side at the bottom, equals the sum of LIABILITIES and EQUITY which appear on the right side at the bottom. This matches with the definitions given above.

In addition to the BALANCE SHEET, which shows the status of the company at an instant of time, it is also desirable to have another piece of information, an INCOME STATEMENT, which displays the changes in the company's activities since the previous BALANCE SHEET was prepared. Together, these two statements give a rounded picture of both the company's position and its most recent activities. An INCOME STATEMENT for the XYZ Company is shown below.

Exhibit 5

INCOME STATEMENT

XYZ COMPANY

June 30, 1979

ITEM	AMOUNT	PERCENT
Net Sales	3,992,758	100%
Cost of Goods Sold	2,680,298	67%
Gross Profit	1,312,460	33%
Selling, General, and Administrative Expense	801,395	20%
Depreciation	111,509	3%
Interest Expense	85,274	2%
Income before taxes	314,782	8%
Taxes	163,708	
Income after taxes	150,574	4%
Dividends to stockholders	92,300	
Addition to Retained Earnings	58,274	

The ratios for use in analyzing the company's position and prospects will come from data in both of these documents; the BALANCE SHEET, and the INCOME STATEMENT.

The Current Ratio

As can be seen from the example following, the **CURRENT RATIO** is the ratio between **CURRENT ASSETS** (typified by cash, accounts receivable, and inventory which can be converted into money with relative ease) and **CURRENT LIABILITIES** (typified by accounts payable and short-term borrowings which are due now or in the near future). It should be noted here that current assets, as stated above, is used interchangeably with the term "Working Capital," to which we will refer in later parts of this book.

The Current Ratio

Equation 2: $\dfrac{\text{Current assets}}{\text{Current Liabilities}} \quad \dfrac{2,240,890}{850,691} = 2.63 \text{ to } 1$

This is a measure of the liquidity of the business, or of its ability to pay its debts on time. It would seem from this ratio that the business is reasonably sound. However, the value of inventory can sometimes become questionable.

The Acid Test Ratio

Equation 3:

Cash	177,689
Accounts Receivable	678,279
Total Quick Assets	855,968 = 1.006 to 1
Current Liabilities	850,691

This is an even more stringent measure of the debt payment ability of the business, since the sometimes questionable value of inventory is excluded from consideration as an asset.

This ratio indicates that this business has a fair probability of paying its bills, since the very short-term, relatively liquid assets of cash and accounts receivable are more than sufficient to cover the current liabilities. However, the ratio is close enough to raise serious concern as to the liquidity of Accounts Receivable. With a ratio this close, a small delay in the income flow from Accounts Receivable could cause an immidiate shortage of operating cash.

There are times when customers do not pay their bills promptly, and, in consequence, the business may experience a lack of ready cash to pay its bills when due. An index of this situation is the average length of time an account receivable is outstanding. This is also an indication of liquidity.

The average age of an account receivable is determined by the relationship which follows.

Age of Accounts Receivable

Where:

T_{ar} = Average Age of Accounts Receivable
A_R = Total Acounts Receivable
S_C = Annual Credit Sales

Equation 4:

$$T_{ar} = \frac{365A_r}{S_c}$$

If this age shows any tendency to increase from one period to another, unless the Acid Test Ratio is substantially higher than that shown above, the company may experience cash shortages which could interfere with its ability to pay its own bills.

If the average age of receivables is higher than the company's net payment terms, the company may be acting as an interest-free banker for its customers, and be losing profit as a result.

To determine if a cash-flow problem exists, the average age of accounts payable becomes a useful ratio. This ratio is also useful in judging the credit worthiness of a customer.

Average Age of Accounts Payable

Where:

T_{ap} = Average Age of Accounts Payable
A_P = Accounts Payable
P_U = Annual Purchases

Equation 5:

$$T_{ap} = \frac{365Ap}{Pu}$$

The extent to which this age exceeds the company's net payment period is an indication of cash-flow problems and lateness with some payables, and a possible use of credit from suppliers as a source of additional working capital. While it is axiomatic that to maximize working capital, one should collect quickly and pay slowly, this does not always maximize profits. Discounts for prompt payment often represent a far superior source of profit, as will be discussed later.

Consideration of the meaning of these age equations is considered vital because both involve cost and loss of use of money. Consequently, they will be discussed in more detail in the chapter on Product Velocity, Turnover, and Holding Cost.

Of interest, from an investment point of view, is an examination of how well the stockholders are doing as a return on their investment in the company. As was discussed earlier in the section on setting profit targets, in order to maintain stockholder or ownership interest in continuing the enterprise and to be able to gain added capital as needed, an owner or stockholder should be able to realize at least as good a return on his investment in the enterprise as he could by making any other investment with the same amount of risk. This ratio is determined as follows.

Stockholders' Return on Equity

Equation 6:

$$\frac{\text{Profit after Taxes}}{\text{Total Equity}} = \frac{150,574}{1,796,621} = 8.38\%$$

It should be noted here that in cases where a business has borrowed money for working capital, this same equation should be used, but with total funds employed (Equity plus borrowings), instead of equity alone.

These ratios furnish a good and frequently used means of appraising the overall health of an enterprise. As such, they should be part of the tool kit for any person in business.

A view of the changes in these ratios over a period of time can be highly revealing as to the health of the company, and of its trend toward improvement or decline. To view this trend, however, yearly figures should be converted into a constant value of a dollar as of some selected base year in order to remove the effects of inflation and deflation. This is discussed in more detail in the sections discussing "Trends over Time" and "Dealing With Inflation."

2. WATCHING THE CASH

Having a business which shows a profit at the end of an accounting period is extremely important; yet, many profitable businesses have sunk without a trace because they lacked adequate cash when it was needed. Prudent, careful, thoughtful management of available cash is one of the most important things a manager can do to assure maximum profitability.

Several factors affect the availability of cash. Credit policy, inventory levels, collection of receivables, inventory turnover rates, product velocity, payment policy regarding payables and purchases; all affect the cash level of a business. Paticularly in a new business cash is often limited and careful management of available cash can be critical.

When inventory is purchased, a commitment to spend cash is made. Once the purchase has been paid for, that cash is locked up, unusable, until the items are not only sold, but paid for. This operates very much like one's own check book, in that we must plan to have the money in the bank in time to pay the checks we must write to pay our bills.

Many people lacking experience get the impression that cash flow is simply profit after taxes plus depreciation. Nothing could be further from the truth, insofar as day-to-day operation of a business is concerned. The missing ingredient is time; **WHEN** cash will come in, and **WHEN** it must go out. The timing of incoming cash often gets far out of step with requirements for payments, and to remain in operation, this gap must be filled from cash on hand, or from borrowings. Particularly in businesses with seasonal operations, knowledge of and planning to fill cash needs is vital. We must know not only **HOW MUCH,** but **WHEN.**

To begin such planning, we need to know the average age of receivables, which we learned about in Section 1 of the previous chapter. However, to be more precise (and extra precision is critical in the case of a new business which often is weak in cash), we need to know what percentage of sales is paid for within various periods of time after the sale. This information can be gained from looking at cash sales records and at accounts receivable records. These can be regrouped according to the amount of time elapsing between sale and payment. A history of several months or even years is helpful, if available.

A form such as that shown as Exhibit 6 is very helpful in arranging

Exhibit 6

INCOME FORECAST WORK SHEET

SOURCE	WEEK ENDING:			WEEK ENDING:			WEEK ENDING:		
	Forecast	Actual	Variance	Forecast	Actual	Variance	Forecast	Actual	Variance
TOTAL SALES									
Cash from sales									
(%) From last week									
(%) From 2 weeks ago									
(%) From 3 weeks ago									
(%) From 4 weeks ago									
(%) From 5 weeks ago									
From past due accts.									
From:									
TOTAL CASH INCOME									

SOURCE	WEEK ENDING:			WEEK ENDING:			WEEK ENDING:		
	Forecast	Actual	Variance	Forecast	Actual	Variance	Forecast	Actual	Variance
TOTAL SALES									
Cash from sales									
(%) From last week									
(%) From 2 weeks ago									
(%) From 3 weeks ago									
(%) From 4 weeks ago									
(%) From 5 weeks ago									
From past due accts.									
From:									
TOTAL CASH INCOME									

ROBERT N. HOBBETT

the information so that the cash position and needs of the business are shown.

As can be seen, like a checking account, the cash flow projection begins with an opening balance amounting to the actual cash on hand at the end of the previous accounting period.

To this must be added the income received from sales during previous periods, and that from any cash sales in the present period to arrive at a total cash balance (before expenses).

Against this income must go the required expenses for the period, including payment for purchases, taxes, payrolls, and all the other expenses. Most of these are known, and the remainder can usually be estimated with some degree of accuracy. Actually these expenditures are in two classes; one, those which must be paid by a certain time, such as taxes, insurance premiums, bank loan payments and the like, and those where there is some degree of flexibility in the actual time of payment.

One then can strike a balance to see whether cash is sufficient or whether borrowing is required. This should be done in two steps; first, taking out the mandatory payments to see what balance of cash remains to cover discretionary payments, then scheduling the discretionary payments so as to minimize the extent of any required borrowing.

An actual case will illustrate how this is done. The client, an auto parts retailer, had a situation where an average of 65% of sales were for cash, another 15% were paid within a 10-day discount period, another 10% within 30 days, 6% within 60 days, and the remainder ran 90 to 120 days with about 1% bad accounts.

While the operation was profitable, the handling of cash was poorly done, with the result that there were frequent cases where cash was insufficient to meet obligations in a timely fashion resulting in the client being put on a COD basis by suppliers. The situation was made more critical by the client's desire to maintain a relatively large inventory so as to serve customers well with great availability of parts, and the fact that business was of a seasonal nature, with sales falling off during the winter months.

The client's balance sheet showed a Curent Ratio of 2.06 to 1, which, one would assume, would indicate soundness in the business. However, the Quick Ratio was less than 1, indicating an out-of-balance situation in the components of working capital, with an excessive investment in inventory in comparison with cash and accounts receivable.

Exhibit 7

DISBURSEMENT FORECAST WORK SHEET

WEEK ENDING:		WEEK ENDING		WEEK ENDING:		WEEK ENDING:		WEEK ENDING:	
Identification	Amount	Identification	Amount	Identification	Amount	Identification	Amount	Identification	Amount
WEEK TOTAL		WEEK TOTAL		WEEK TOTAL		WEEK TOTAL		WEEK TOTAL	

ROBERT N. HORBETT

This resulted, of course, in an excessive dependence on prompt collections in order to have cash to meet payments when due.

As is often the case, this situation had been going on for some period of time, and, as a result, the working cash had declined to a grave level, often insufficient. Because of this critical imbalance in the business, it was decided to make projections weekly until cash from profits could be accumulated to permit longer period projections.

Simultaneously an analysis of inventory turnover was begun with the purpose of eliminating slow-moving items so as to bring inventory, accounts receivable, and cash into better balance by reducing the amount of cash locked up in inventory, and reducing the cost of holding that inventory by increasing the turnover rate and decreasing the length of time a given item remained in inventory.

As preparation for the cash flow forecast, a schedule of payables (DISBURSEMENTS) was prepared, in the form shown on the preceding page. The various items are described, and the amounts are entered under the week in which they should be paid.

The actual cash flow forecast is done in several steps, shown as Exhibit 8.

1. The balance of cash on hand and in the bank is entered in the first line of the first column.
2. Income from sales in past periods is entered in the second, third, fourth, and fifth lines of the first column.
3. Income from cash sales from the present week is entered.
4. The expected income from accounts receivable is posted to the week in which payment could be expected.
5. A total of available cash at week end is posted.
6. A total of expenditures for the current period is taken from the Disbursement Forecast Work Sheet (Exhibit 10).
7. A new balance of cash on hand is determined.

If this balance turns out to be negative (if there is not to be enough cash to meet the scheduled payables) then management must pay only what it can and defer the remainder. Consequently, a search must be made of the Payables Work Sheet to select deferrable items, which then should be transferred to the next or another column of the Payables Work Sheet appropriate to the planned date of payment. This is often the case in small businesses, as it was with the client under dis-

Exhibit 8

CASH FLOW FORECAST SUMMARY SHEET

ITEM	WEEK ENDING:			WEEK ENDING:			WEEK ENDING:		
	Forecast	Actual	Variance	Forecast	Actual	Variance	Forecast	Actual	Variance
Beginning Balance									
Income									
Adjustments to income									
Sub-total									
Disbursements									
Balance forward									

ITEM	WEEK ENDING:			WEEK ENDING:			WEEK ENDING:		
	Forecast	Actual	Variance	Forecast	Actual	Variance	Forecast	Actual	Variance
Beginning Balance									
Income									
Adjustments to income									
Sub-total									
Disbursements									
Balance forward									

ROBERT N. HOBBETT

cussion. If the totals of items which could be deferred without protest from the supplier still leaves a shortage of cash, then the only choices left to management are to borrow from a bank or from a private source, to plead with suppliers for longer payment terms, or to declare bankruptcy.

In marginal cases, people in business often write checks to satisfy payables when they really do not have the money in the bank, in the hope that by the time the check reaches the bank, they will have received sufficient added income to make the check good.

This is a hazardous procedure at best, and can subject the owner or manager to fines and jail terms if it fails. One should be aware that the banking system is exerting very strenuous efforts to reduce the time required for a check to be cleared through the banking system and be paid from the customer's account.

If borrowing becomes necessary, as is often the case in seasonal businesses, a point of major concern to both bank and borrower is when the borrowing will be repaid. A cash-flow projection such as the foregoing will give both parties something fairly concrete upon which to frame the terms of the loan, with some degree of confidence that they can be met.

A borrower can be certain that a lender will have little interest in meeting the borrower's needs unless he is quite convinced that his investment will be returned. Again, the conservative perceptions of risk usually adopted by lenders can be counteracted by careful presentations of forecasts, conservative in formulation, and well documented. Again, this is another aspect of the difficulty of borrowing for a new enterprise without a well-established and favorable track record.

The other side of the coin is the investment of surplus cash. There should be no more cash kept idle in the business than is necessary to meet day-to-day operating needs. Any cash beyond this point should be invested and be kept working to produce income. Although short-term investments rarely offer a high rate of return without a correspondingly high level of risk, any return whatsoever is better than no return at all on the idle funds.

Interest-bearing savings accounts are a first level for this, although they pay the lowest interest rates. Investment in treasury securities, notes, bonds, commercial paper, and money-market funds are all additional vehicles for investment. With careful planning of disbursements, surplus cash can be put out to work, on a planned maturity basis so that it becomes available when needed to meet disbursement needs.

An important item to remember is that for its owners, a business exists to make a profit, and that the essential of the operation is the manipulation and use of money to gain a profit. The type of business, and the demands for special trade knowledge, training, and expeience, although all too often viewed as primary objectives, **are truly secondary to the profit requirement, and the type of business or profession selected is only the chosen vehicle by which the manipulation and use of money for profit is accomplished.**

3. COST-PROFIT-VOLUME ANALYSIS

As business people, we intuitively feel that the amount of business we do should directly affect the amount of profit we earn; more volume, larger profits, and the reverse. Although this sometimes does not happen in real life, we usually feel that it should. And when it does not happen, we become quite disturbed, as well we should. As modern phraseology would put it, we expect a linear relationship to exist between volume and profits.

Of course, we cannot achieve profits until our costs have been paid; all of them! (This, sometimes, through wishful thinking, manages to escape the notice of some owners or managers.) But whether we like it or not, this is what really must happen.

Costs can be divided into two broad classes with which we must deal, each in a different way. The first class consists of all the moneys we must spend to make and sell a product, or to render a service, which rise and fall with how much we make or how much service we render, and which do not occur except when we actually make something or render a service.

These costs are directly related to a unit of product or a unit of service, and have a first claim on any money we have on hand, or get from our customers. Without spending this money, we would have nothing to sell. We will label this type of cost as **VARIABLE COST, since all costs of this type will vary with the level of our productive activity.**

The second class of costs is that group of costs which are associated with the decisions of management, including the basic decision to be in that particular business at that place and time. **We label these costs MANAGEMENT COSTS.**

These costs are usually not related to the volume of business done (except in extreme cases which we will discuss specifically later), and almost always are a function of the passage of time. They continue to occur, regardless of minor changes in the volume of productive activity. Also included in this class of cost are the cost effects of any general inefficiencies or suboptimal policies which management may have tolerated, or placed in effect.

It should be noted here that in extreme cases, where the enterprise undertakes a major expansion or contraction, quantum jumps will take place in the level of Management Costs. Such changes are a true province of management decision, and, as such, are within the class of costs which should be chargeable to management. However, they are not within the ebb and flow of everyday activity with which the typical manager must deal.

Clearly, then, these costs should not be associated with the actual production of a particular product or service, but rather with the generalized cost of being there, ready to do business.

In a continuing business operation in which sales are being made and money is being spent to accomplish the necessary work, there are some fundamental financial relationships which are very useful to remember. As is the case in many other situations, these relationships are best shown as equations, with symbols to denote each of the variables. Of course, when we use equations, it is first necessary to define what each of those symbols means.

The Business Equation

Where: S = Sales Income
   V = Variable Costs
   M = Management Costs
   P = Profit
   $(?)$ = "We Hope!"

Equation 8: $S = V + M + P \ (?)$

Since Variable Costs represent money already spent for the goods and services sold, these costs have a first claim on any sales income. Then, of course, the Management Costs for the period must be recovered before there can be any profit. This is the reason for the special little "We Hope!" symbol (indicating some uncertainty) after the "P" for Profit in this equation.

Another new term which we will find extremely useful is that which we will label **CONTRIBUTION RATIO,** for which we shall use the symbol "R." It is defined by means of the following equation.

Contribution Ratio

Where C = Contribution
      R = Contribution Ratio

Equation 9:
$$R = \frac{S - V}{S} = \frac{M + P}{S} = \frac{C}{S}$$

This establishes the **CONTRIBUTION RATIO** as the **percentage of the monetary unit of sales which is available for Management Costs and Profit after Variable Costs have been paid.** It is important to note here that **CONTRIBUTION** (C) and its **CONTRIBUTION RATIO (R) may apply to an establishment as a whole, or to any component of it,** such as a specific division, product, or profit center within the enterprise.

This concept will be of particular importance in using cost-profit-volume analysis as a diagnostic tool for management guidance.

The relationship between these variables is sometimes easier to see and understand if expressed as a graph or picture. One follows below. You will note that at the point of zero sales on the graph, the profit path crosses the profit axis at a point well below the horizontal zero profit line. The diagram labels this intercept as Management Cost. This may seem a bit strange, but what it really tells us is that the Management Costs for any period will be a loss until paid for from the accumulated contribution of a series of sales. We will deal with the uses of this concept later on. (See Eq. 8)

Examination of cost-volume-profit behavior of a going enterprise can be an extremely useful diagnostic tool, as we shall soon see. The first procedure to be considered is the determination of the existing profit

Exhibit 9

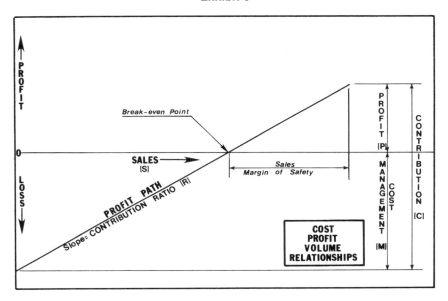

Exhibit 10

MONTH	COMPANY A		COMPANY B	
	Sales	Profit	Sales	Profit
1.	11,300	1,000	57,142	15,430
2.	13,460	1,496	63,475	9,478
3.	9,750	475	78,675	19,635
4.	8,560	(130)	84,630	15,468
5.	9,300	225	126,545	35,780
6.	10,425	730	97,630	18,963
7.	14,675	1,960	100,465	31,463
8.	13,460	1,865	82,640	18,975
9.	11,223	890	77,635	16,876
10.	10,325	675	62,940	15,340
11.	12,672	1,475	25,360	(3,760)
12.	9,680	440	22,478	(2,045)
13.	8,750	79	30,160	1,500
14.	9,635	395	45,900	7,593
15.	10,140	497	48,765	3,628
16.	12,835	1,517	65,400	13,683
17.	14,247	1,896	72,800	15,496
18.	15,620	2,518	47,300	6,560
Totals	200,057	16,643	1,144,940	205,233
Averages	11,448	925	63,608	11,402

SALES AND PROFITS

path of the enterprise; that is, how profits behave with changes in sales volume.

The simplest way of making the initial examination is to make a graphic plot of net profits before taxes versus net sales in monetary units, working from a set of monthly profit-and-loss statements, putting a dot on the chart at each point which represents a month's combination of sales and profit (or loss).

There is always a question as to how much data should be included in such an examination. There is a conflict between the desirability of having much data so as to be sound statistically, and the fact that if we reach too far into the past, things will have changed too much to make sound comparisons. Usually, the most recent twelve to eighteen months proves satisfactory.

The resulting pattern of dots (or even the lack of a pattern) can be very revealing. In most circumstances, the dots will tend to string out in a direction from low left to high right, indicating that as sales increase, profits increase. This pattern is indicative of the general profit path of the enterprise.

Failure of a reasonably clear pattern of this nature to appear is an immediate indication of the existence of some quite serious problem, which will be discussed in detail in later paragraphs. Minor conditions will always cause a certain amount of scattering around the average profit path and the degree or extent of scattering can also be very revealing, as we shall discuss.

Listed above as Exhibit 10 are the sales and profit data from two different companies, covering a period of eighteen months of operation. We shall use this information in several different ways to examine the health of each of these two companies and to see what the data can tell us about them.

A visual scan of these two sets of data does not reveal much detail such as would furnish firm guidance for management decisions. However, when the data are plotted in graph form, we can begin to see some interesting things.

In Exhibit 11 below, showing the behavior pattern of Company A, one can see a clear trend; so clear, in fact, that one may gain a close approximation of the profit path by passing a straight edge or stretching a rubber band along the pattern of points, averaging out the number of points on either side of the straight edge, and noting where that line would cross the sales axis and the profit axis. The "rubber-band

Exhibit 11

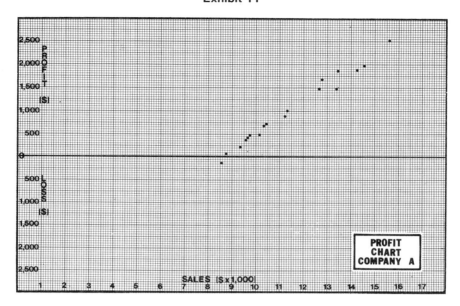

method" of approximating the profit path or other trends is a very useful and quick method for use in preliminary discussion and planning.

This may be compared with Exhibit 12 which shows the profit behavior pattern of Company B. One can see from the numerical data that Company B enjoys a much larger sales volume than Company A. However, the graphical plot below shows that its pattern of profits is much more erratic, as can be seen from the distinctly wider scattering of the plotted points.

Causes for this erratic departure from pattern are discussed in detail in Chapter 5, Section 2.

To obtain more accurate results, particularly in cases where a substantial amount of scatter is present, the mathematical techniques of regression become useful, as with forecasting. Details of how to calculate regressions are given in the Appendix, Section 1, as well as calculations for the Coefficient of Correlation. These, together with the Standard Deviation, covered in Chapter 5, Section 3, give quantitative measures of scatter.

Exhibit 12

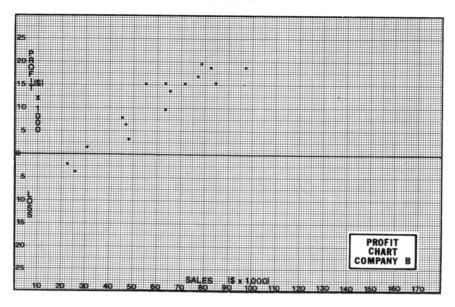

Exhibits 13 and 14 exemplify application of regression techniques to the establishment of profit paths. The profit paths have simply been plotted on top of the scattergrams of data points previously shown.

Now we can begin to see some pattern. Company A had a contribution ratio of 34% of sales, while Company B showed 36%. These levels of the contribution ratio are average to low for typical business.

A high contribution ratio would seem to be desirable, and is often seen in new, faddish or suddenly popular items. Actually, it is not as desirable as it may seem, if there is any amount of variation in sales volume from one accounting period to another.

Let us assume that we were to have an extremely good contribution ratio, for example, 85%. In the U.S.A., this would mean that for each gain or loss of only one dollar in sales, our profit would rise or fall by 85¢. If we were to have any volatility at all in sales volume, our profit position would be highly variable, and vulnerable to small decreases in sales volume.

A highly volatile level of profits from one period to another can, perhaps, be explained to knowledgeable shareholders with relative ease. Nonetheless, unless preparations are made in advance, a manage-

Exhibit 13

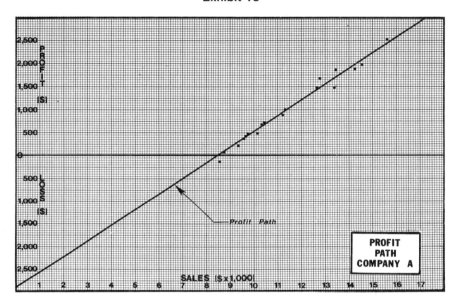

Exhibit 14

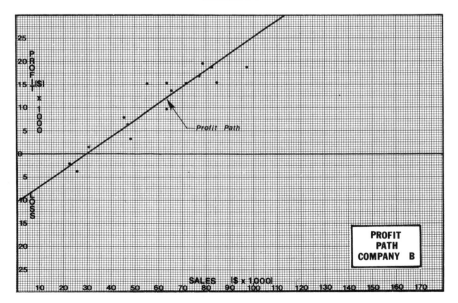

ment can be seriously embarrassed by a sudden minor fall in sales, producing a serious and unexpected decline in the level of profits.

This is perhaps an item of greater concern to the larger (perhaps publicly held) company than to the small one, particularly if the small one is closely held, as is often the case. Even then, however, such volatility can cause difficulties for a company which has become accustomed to the good times, and fails to take potential declines into consideration in planning.

On the other hand, if we were to seek real stability of profits, we would lower the contribution ratio. A shift too far in this direction and we find ourselves making a noncompetitive return and losing investors. The range of 30 to 45% seems to represent the most acceptable compromise between high earnings, and stability of profits over time for most companies.

Break-even calculations are particularly easy using the relations given previously. Management Costs divided by the Contribution Ratio (expressed as a decimal) give the precise value, as seen in the following equation.

Break-Even Determination

Where:

S_{be} = Sales at Break-even Point

Equation 10:

$$S_{be} = \frac{M}{R}$$

Usually, the variable cost of a product or service is the easiest type of cost to determine, which facilitates solutions of the pricing problem.

More importantly, calculation of the required sales volume which will be needed to satisfy some selected profit target is equally easy. In Chapter 3 entitled Setting Profit Targets, we discussed ways of determining the minimum profit we should require, in terms of return on funds employed under the existing conditions of risk. This can be converted to a total sum of pretax profits required to which must be added the Management Costs for the period under consideration in order to obtain the total Contribution required. This, divided by the Contribution Ratio (R) will yield the target sales level which should give the targeted profit if achieved. The following equation governs.

Sales Target

Where:

S_t = Target Sales
P_t = Target Profit
M = Management costs for the period
R = Contribution Ratio

Equation 11:

$$S_t = \frac{M + P_t}{R}$$

Another problem area for operating management is the common accounting practice of "Whole Costing." The principle invoked is that each unit of production should bear its "Whole Cost" including its portion of Management Costs. In theory, there seems to be nothing wrong about this, for the Management Costs must be recovered somehow before any profit can be gained.

In practice, however, this can result in deceptive figures unless adjustments are made. To allocate period or Management Costs over units of production or sales requires the making of an advance assumption as to the volume of activity over which the management costs are to be allocated.

If any other volume of activity is reached than that used as a basis for allocation, the resulting profits will be more or less than predicted, due to over- or under-absorption of the Management Costs. This is usually taken care of by means of an adjustment on the bottom of the Income Statement, but this is of little help to the operating manager, who must look first at the Cost of Goods Sold, and thus can be misled.

Whole costing is required by present tax legislation, because it "shows the real value" of work in process; i.e., the work sitting unfinished at the end of an accounting period should be charged a proportional amount of the management costs for the period.

To illustrate the confusing effects of overhead application to pricing and profit planning by means of conventional "whole costing" principles, let us develop an example.

Let us assume that there is a small home builder who is trying to price some work. The house-building picture doesn't look promising for next year, so he plans to go into remodeling. Hd looks at the previous year, and finds that he built and sold two houses.

Sale of two houses	$150,000	100%
Labor, Material, and Direct Expense	97,500	65%
Contribution (Gross Profit)	$ 52,500	35%
Overhead*	37,500	25%
Profit	15,000	10%

* Overhead consists of depreciation, office costs, salaries of owner and full-time employees, accounting services, and the other things necessary to keeping a business open and ready to operate. We will not use this term elsewhere, for it has too many different meanings to various people.

Since he is careful to make complete and detailed estimates, our builder can get a good fix for estimating the direct labor, material, and direct expense on future jobs. He determined his combined overhead and profit rate as a percentage of labor and material used.

This turns out to be:

$$\frac{\$52,500}{\$97,500} = 53.846\%$$

So, he needed to add $.53846 to each dollar of labor, material, and expense to determine his selling price. Being pretty good with numbers, he decides to use a multiplier of 1.53846 for all his costs to reach a selling price.

He then quoted and got a series of jobs in which he expected to spend $81,250 for labor, material, and expense, and the total quoted was $125,000. He naturally expected $12,500 profit from the work, which took a year to do, and was extremely upset when his accountant told him he only made $6,250 for the year. (See case I following.)

He went over his estimates, and carefully checked his overhead rate. Yes, he had done his arithmetic correctly. He looked at his job sheets. He had hit every job on the nose. No excess cost there! But where did his other $6,250 go that he expected but didn't have? He thought,

"Maybe I didn't do enough business. What would have happened if I had done some more jobs?"

So he added in another couple of jobs that he didn't get, just to see what would have happened. These two jobs would have added another $31,200 to his labor and material cost, for a total of $112,450, which he marked up to $173,000. He went back to his accountant, and said, "If I had done $173,000 of business, I would have made $17,300. Right?"

The accountant said, "Wrong!" After working over the figures a moment, he said, "You would have made $23,050."

"But that's crazy. First you tell me I made less than I expected, then, with a little more business, you tell me I made more than I expected. I didn't change the overhead rate, and I didn't spend any more or less money on the office or on my salary! I made sure I absorbed all my costs when I set up the overhead rate."

The accountant said, "Well, here is what happened," and wrote down the results.

CASE 1

Sales	$125,000
Labor, Material, and Expense	81,250
Contribution	$ 43,750
Overhead	37,500
Profit	$ 6,250

CASE 2

Sales	$173,000
Labor, Material, and Expense	112,450
Contribution	$ 60,550
Overhead	37,500
Profit	$ 23,050

"If you had sold $150,000, you would have come out as planned. But you didn't. Yet the actual overhead was still spent even though the allocation by overhead rate didn't really cover it. You under-absorbed your overhead. In the second case, you sold a lot more, so there was more in the kitty for overhead, but you didn't spend anymore, so you over-absorbed your overhead."

The builder went away mumbling to himself.

The real answer to this kind of situation is not to use an overhead rate at all. Management costs will go on pretty much without change so long as the business operates, and without much regard to what volume of business is done (within the normal range of ebb and flow).

Many Management Costs are determined by the business environment at the chosen location. As soon as the decision is made to enter business at a location, Management is locked in with these costs.

In this case, labor, material, and direct expense (total variable cost) constituted 65% of sales, yielding a contribution of 35%. This, after deducting "overhead" (Management Costs) yielded a satisfactory profit on the basis of past experience.

As we mentioned previously, a Contribution Ratio in the range of 30% to about 45% is about par for most businesses. Therefore, if you divide your dollar estimate for labor, material, and direct expense by its own percentage of sales (as a decimal) you will get a price which will return you the scheduled contribution. If the contribution ratio isn't large enough, select one which will suit, and price accordingly. It operates by this formula.

Pricing Equation

Where:

S_u = Selling price per unit
V_u = Variable cost per unit
R_t = Target Contribution Ratio (as a decimal)

Equation 12:

$$S_u = \frac{V_u}{1 - R_t}$$

It is very important to note that this procedure will only yield a target price which will return the required Contribution per unit if the costs are accurate. This does not say whether or not that price will be acceptable to the customers, or that it will be competitive. This must be tested.

If the price so determined is too high to be competitive, management then has a choice of either decreasing the price and lowering the Contribution to be received from the sale, or of refusing to make the sale.

Conversely, if a price better than the one which was targeted can be realized in the marketplace, then it certainly should be used in the interest of maximizing profit.

What is really being said here is that in our interest in precision and in making use of advanced methods, we must not lose sight of the realities of the marketplace.

If we were to have a marginal business with a poor margin of safety, what can we do about it from a management point of view? A number of ways exist to improve the margin of safety, and we shall explore all of them. These measures may be used singly or in combination, and how best this may be done will depend upon the particular circumstances of the business under examination.

1. The attempt can be made to simply sell more at existing prices and terms. This is somewhat an unreal expectation, for such an attempt almost always brings added costs, the effects of which must be considered in reaching any decision.

2. An attempt can be made to reduce variable costs. This is likely to be the most fruitful approach in an industrialized economy, as it furnishes the greatest opportunity for application of ingenuity in reduction of human effort. This has the effect of improving the Contribution Ratio and thereby increasing the probability of profit at any sales level.

3. An attempt can be made to reduce Management Costs. This should always be a matter of importance; however, many Management Costs become truly fixed, or beyond the control of management once the decision to be in that business at that time and place has been implemented. Although the opportunities for reduction of costs are limited in this area, they are also insidious, creeping in undetected unless carefully monitored. Policing these costs is a constant task of management.

4. Prices can be increased. This method is placed last in the array of possibilities, since it should be considered a matter of last resort. In a competitive situation, the leaders in increasing prices also increase their exposure to losses in business volume through price

competition, unless there is some sort of monopoly or cartel in existence. A business which can successfully cut its costs is in a far better position to maintain profitability in the face of price competition than one which cannot or will not, since it can lead its competitors, and still maintain profits.

When considering a situation in which a number of different products or services may be involved, management often needs enlightenment as to relative profitability and of areas of problems. A very good source of such guidance is through use of the comparative Contribution Ratios of the products or services.

Naturally, one should seek to improve the overall profitability of the enterprise by improving the total Contribution Ratio (within whatever constraints of profit stability may exist). Very often, particularly when records are not well kept as is often the case in the smaller company, there will be one or more products or services which are not making the appropriate amount of contribution to profit.

This may come about through the force of competition, or through bargaining with customers, but in any case, needs immediate attention. Often, such situations arise from the self-serving activities of salesmen paid a commission on the total monetary value of their sales. Their personal objective then becomes one of maximizing their own sales volume without regard to the profitability of their efforts. American sales managers as well as salesmen are often guilty of being unduly impressed by sheer volume.

The relative strength and contribution of various products and services to the welfare of the enterprise can be shown graphically by means of a "hip roof chart" such as that shown as Exhibit 15 below. In constructing this chart, items are arranged in descending order of their Contribution Ratio, and each is shown with its total Contribution for the period under study.

We call the chart a "Hip Roof" Chart because when it is plotted, the contribution lines for the various products or profit centers resemble the changing angles of the hip roof on a barn.

Once individual Contribution Ratios have been derived for each product or service, management has several available areas of specific action and decision, and in this respect, can gain a more precise level of guidance for actions designed to improve the margin of safety.

By visual examination, and even the "rubber band technique," the

Exhibit 15

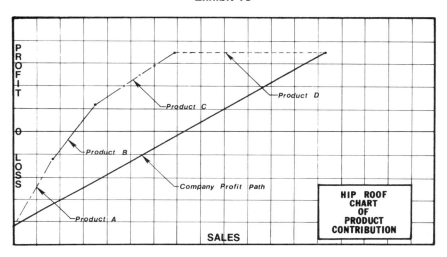

approximate effects of various sales and cost reduction strategies can be seen and appraised, and management can see more accurately where attention is most needed.

1. *Items of* **LOW** *Contribution Ratio:*

    a. Consideration should be given as to whether or not sale of the products or services in question should be discontinued. At times, eliminating a product or service will relieve facilities, equipment, and manpower to be devoted to more profitable items. At times, also, continuation of sales is felt to be necessary in order to promote the sale of some other, more profitable items. This situation often needs careful examination and test to assure that it is indeed true. Often, a strategy of benign neglect of sales effort for that item will effect the necessary proof.

    b. If the product or service truly must be continued, management has a specific point for application of cost reduction efforts, or as a last resort, increasing prices.

2. *Items of* **HIGH** *Contribution Ratio:*

    a. Often an increase in sales effort and in the advertising budget will favorably affect the sales volume of these items.

    b. Consideration should also be given to the relative price elasticity of the item. If the item is price sensitive, a small price reduction may prove to be highly profitable through a large increase in sales volume. This possibility should be carefully examined and tested.

The Hip Roof technique has other uses than merely comparing products or services. By appropriate accounting breakdowns, it can be used to compare departments, cost centers, or even different divisions of the operation. With such broad utility, it becomes a very useful tool for management to use in forward planning.

By looking at Exhibit 15, we can see that the company would be considerably better off if the sales of Product "D" were to be discontinued. Profits would remain relatively unchanged, the unprofitable money trading involved in product "D" would be eliminated, and the margin of safety of the company would be improved. Capacity previously devoted to product "D" could then be devoted to the production of some new, and probably more profitable item. If, for some reason, Product "D" must be retained, it becomes an immediate and direct target for cost reduction efforts.

Product "A" is a worthy candidate for expanded sales, if at all possible. Certainly, efforts should be made in that direction, and the Contribution Ratio, as one can see from the steepness of the line, is strong enough to accept some reduction in price without undue harm if volume could be substantially increased thereby. Possibly the best improvement would be to substitute expanded production of product "A" for product "D." This, too, should be explored thoroughly.

An unexplored area of strategy for profit improvement under special conditions is that of the short-term use of excess capacity. It must be remembered that **after the break-even point has been reached and management costs for the period have been recovered, the entire contribution from each additional monetary unit of sales is pure pre-income tax profit.**

Therefore, if operations are below capacity, and additional business can be secured which will yield any amount of contribution at all, and if this business can be completed either within the remainder of the accounting period, or in such manner as not to interfere with the production of more profitable items, efforts should certainly be made to secure that extra business.

Whatever additional contribution so produced is additional profit which otherwise would not have been obtained.

It is important to stress again the above-mentioned limitations on use of this strategy. This is a short-term, "in and out" type of strategy, which will harm the business if allowed to interfere with the acquisition of more profitable longer term commitments from customers.

A direct example of the results of hip-roof analysis comes from the case of a modestly sized manufacturer of fractional horsepower motors some years ago. The company was showing few profits and occasional losses; a decidedly marginal situation, which seriously disturbed the company's Board of Directors. A consultant was requested to study the situation.

A hip-roof study was therefore made, and the result was very enlightening. It happened that more than half of the company's sales volume was derived from sales of wiper, window, and seat motors to the auto industry.

The study revealed that on these motors, the company was not even recovering its variable costs, let alone achieving any contribution to management costs or to profit, and that sales of other motors were sustaining the company against this drag.

The recommendation was therefore made to discontinue further sales of these types of motors until the Engineering Department could redesign them to become cost effective and competitive at a normal yield. The recommendation was bitterly fought by the sales personnel, but was finally adopted by the Directors. The next year the company paid its first dividend in ten years, and since that time, has been operating quite profitably.

4. ANALYZING COST BEHAVIOR

Additional guidance for management may also be obtained from detailed examination of the behavior of each individual expense account with variations in the level of sales. In an earlier chapter, we mentioned that there were two types of cost or expense: Variable and Management.

Exhibit 16 below shows the typical pattern of behavior of an item of Variable Expense with changes in the volume of sales or productive activity. As we previously saw in the case of profit charts, there is apt to be some degree of scatter, indicating the presence of some errors, random variations, or the operation of one or more outside factors other than the volume of activity.

Exhibit 16

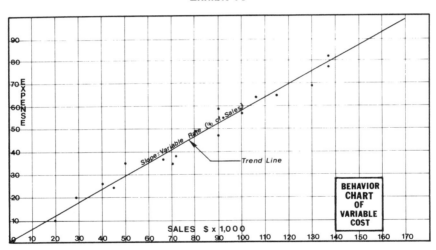

Exhibit 17 below shows the typical behavior of a Management cost item. Again, some scatter is likely to be found. In Chapter 5, Sections 3 and 4, we will discuss the causes of scatter, and its interpretation in terms of quantitative statements of uncertainty. However, to do so, it is again necessary to apply regression methods to establish the average relationship between cost and activity, and to establish the measure of relationship by means of the Coefficient of Correlation and the Standard Deviation as will be discussed.

Exhibit 17

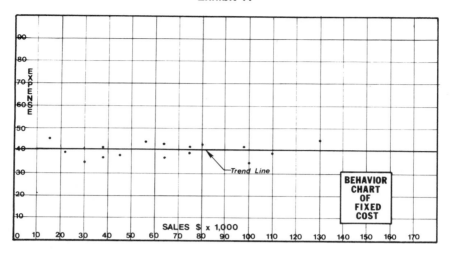

In addition to these two clear types of behavior, there is also a mixture of the two which often occurs. As seen in Exhibit 18 below, there seems to be a variable component which rises and falls with productive activity, and a residual level of ongoing cost which remains even at the zero point of activity.

It is important to note here some things which are frequently done in conventional accounting practice and which can cause problems for the operating manager.

There is the practice of arbitrarily dividing cost accounts into two classifications; Cost of Goods Sold, which is usually assumed to be a variable, and General and Administrative Expense, which is usually assumed to be fixed, although neither situation is truly descriptive of what actually occurs in practice.

When actual behavior is examined, there are often fixed residuals in some components of the Cost of Goods Sold which should properly be placed in Management Costs. Conversely, there are sometimes variable components to items customarily allocated to General and Administrative Expense. These components actually belong in Variable Cost.

As a result of the behavior of some of these mixed or "semivariable" accounts, both Cost of Goods Sold and General and Administrative Costs can be misstated. A more precise policy when mixed behavior is

Exhibit 18

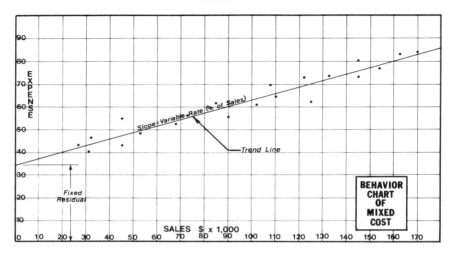

found would be to establish two separate accounts for the fixed and the variable portions of these mixed accounts, so that each component, either fixed or variable, could be applied properly in accord with actual behavior to establish a truer Variable and a truer Management Cost.

In fairness to the accounting profession, they are more often right than wrong in their preconceived classifications, and it becomes extremely useful to inquire as to the reason whenever an account behaves differently from what would normally be expected; even though one should not develop an iron-bound conviction that any account must behave only in some preconceived manner. The reason for unexpected behavior may be valid, or it may indicate some waste or other profit-decreasing condition which should require management attention. Only careful inquiry and evaluation will make such a determination.

Even more serious, at least potentially, is the impact of application of "Whole Costing" principles on the pricing of new and untried products and services. For such items, without any history of behavior, the probable error involved in making the necessary assumption as to sales volume or in the application of fixed "overhead" or "burden" rates is much higher. Such a situation advances the possibility that management might adopt a completely wrong production and marketing strategy, with possibly fatal consequences. An example was shown earlier in the case of the building contractor.

Two examples of this possibility occurred in the auto industry; the pricing of the Airstream models by Chrysler, and of the Edsel by Ford. Failure to attain the predicted sales volume nearly wrecked both companies.

One can also ascribe these problems to poor market analysis or poor marketing techniques. These will be discussed in later chapters. However, if sound cost information and estimates does not reach those who make the pricing and marketing decisions, the chance for serious, perhaps fatal error is greatly increased.

A further note should be added regarding the amount of scatter found in the analysis of each individual expense account. If scatter is large, and the Coefficient of Correlation (See Chapter 5, Section 2 for details) is low, it could well indicate that a cost is actually out of control.

There are some exceptions that can occur, particularly in the case of legal and professional expenses, which will vary in a completely unpredictable fashion. Under present conditions, one cannot predict being sued, having to file suit, or having to prepare testimony or copies of documents demanded by some government agency which are not in the regular line of work. In normal profit planning, a contingency allowance should be made for these unanticipated events.

5. Interpretation and Diagnosis

1. VERIFYING COSTS

It is important to verify the level of management costs indicated by regression analysis as discussed previously. The intercept of Management Cost found by regressing profits against sales is essentially a statistical average of existing behavior, and, while it is often highly indicative, it should not be accepted without test. Errors or arbitrary accounting assumptions can cause confusion.

The total of all accounts showing pure fixed behavior, together with the sum of the fixed residuals from all the mixed accounts, should closely aproximate the management costs shown through regression. If correspondence between these two items is not close, investigation should be made of cost reporting and accounting procedures and of potential sources of error to eliminate this problem.

Very often, the Management Costs shown by regression as mentioned in Chapter 4, Section 3, are found to be considerably higher than management expects them to be. This results from the fact that the regression is an expression of real average behavior, and will include the cost of any inefficiencies or suboptimal policies which existing management may have established, or even merely condoned through neglect. Detailed investigation is needed in such case.

The sum of the various true variables (determined by account analysis) and the variable components of mixed accounts, (when converted into a percentage of sales), should correspond closely with a value derived by subtracting the Contribution Ratio (as a decimal value, resulting from the earlier regression of profits on sales) from one (1.00). This gives a cross-check on the total variable cost as a percentage of sales.

It is also very important to question the cause of any mixed behavior in accounts which should be entirely variable. In numerous cases, items like indirect labor, material handling cost, shipping, and other indirect items of expense show fixed residuals indicative of some type of waste or sub-optimal policies which have been established or tolerated by management.

In so doing, however, preconceptions can lead to serious error if they are not justified by factual analysis. Typically, in manufacturing, direct labor is a pure variable cost. When production falls off, production workers are laid off. When production requirements increase, more workers are hired.

Typical of such apparently sub-optimal policies would be that of retaining the members of a trained work crew during temporary slack times. This is a management decision, and the cost should properly be charged to management costs. Yet such a decision may be quite proper in light of the need to preserve the value of the investment in training the crew, even though the crew is not momentarily productive. Consequently costs are higher than they could be, on a short-term basis.

A similar case might be that of retaining employees nearing retirement, even though their effectiveness has declined. This is a social decision, affecting the company image, and could be quite appropriate in management's judgment. Yet, the decision does increase costs above the lowest level, and should be charged to management.

In any case, when things do not appear as you think they should, careful and thorough investigation without prejudice should be made.

For example, a fixed residual in the direct labor account would certainly not be wrong in a department store or other retail establishment. Although the number of clerks is normally increased during busy seasons, there is often a minimum number which must be present for the store to open, regardless of whether or not any sales are made. In such circumstances, existence of a fixed residual component in the Direct Labor account would be entirely in order, although its magnitude should be checked for real need.

In any event, the underlying reasons for account behavior should be investigated until they are thoroughly understood, and costs should be controlled accordingly.

2. CAUSES FOR SCATTER

Although we expect a clear relationship between profit and volume to exist, there are a number of reasons why a strict profit-volume relationship will not always be clearly shown in a plot of profits versus sales, or in plots of expense behavior versus sales. A number of prominent causes are detailed below. It should be noted, however, that these factors may operate singly, or in any sort of combination, and that this list is far from complete as compared with the problems that may occur in the field.

There is, first and foremost, the problem of the accuracy of the records. Inaccuracies and posting errors can cause poor results and excessive scatter. And such errors will occur !

Second, there is actual random variation of costs due to minor changes from one month to another. Normally, this should be minor, but if excessive, the cause should be investigated.

Third is the practice of Cash instead of Accrual accounting frequently adopted by small business people. Cash Accounting places total receipts and expenditures in the months in which they were made, regardless of whether this truly reflects the situation or not. In the case of expenditures such as insurance premiums, often paid for a whole year in advance, Cash Accounting puts the entire premium as a cost to the month in which paid, while other periods, while benefiting from the insurance, bear none of the cost. This seriously distorts the profit-volume relationship.

Actually, such a payment is an asset (prepaid expense) which is used up gradually over the entire period for which the payment was made (a year). If handled by Cash Accounting, the month in which the premium was paid is severely penalized, and the next eleven months are unduly inflated. Accrual accounting would spread the premium over the entire year, and balance out the cost equally among the months benefited by the expenditure.

Fourth, scatter will occur when there is a range of products or services with different contribution ratios, and the mix of products or services changes from one month to another. If, in one month, only items of high contribution ratio are sold, profits may be quite good. On the other hand, if in another month the same total dollar volume were to be sold and the items were all of low contribution ratio, the company's profits could be much lower, and it might even show a loss.

Fifth, scatter often shows itself in the case of a new product or service, or in the contracting or job-shop type of operation in which cost controls are weak, and/or cost estimating is uncertain. When costs are constantly under- or overrunning estimates, particularly when "Whole Costing" is used with its arbitrary burden rates, scatter can become sufficiently severe to make profits completely unpredictable, because of the impact of cost uncertainties on bidding and pricing. Many job shops and contractors have been destroyed because of excessively low prices based on inadequate cost estimates or poor control of costs.

Sixth, scatter can be caused by lag time between the incurring of expense and the selling of the goods for which the expense was incurred. This often happens in cases of slow inventory turn-over or long processing times, particularly when prices and costs are fluctuating rapidly.

The extent to which this may exist can be tested by regressing current sales against expenses incurred in successive previous months. These may be compared and appropriate lag time selected by calculating and comparing the Coefficient of Correlation for each regression, and selecting the expense period which yields the highest Coefficient of Correlation.

Pricing without reference to true total costs can be a yawning trap for the unwary. It is a common tendency in developing small business to attempt to buy one's way into a competitive market with low prices. Such prices may be adequate to sustain the individual proprietor when working alone, but rapidly become inadequate when the business grows in size and employment.

The Coefficient of Correlation measures the degree of association between the two variables, (in this case, sales and expense), and ranges from $+1.00$ indicating perfect direct association, through 0 indicating no association at all, to -1.00 indicating perfect inverse association. See Appendix, Section 6 for details and formulas.

The existence of scatter where there should be little or none is generally a symptom of something unusual happening; intrusion of some outside factor, or some source of error. In any case, investigation is in order, because scatter represents uncertainty, and with high scatter, prediction and planning for the future becomes very uncertain.

A question arises as to how much scatter is excessive. While hard boundaries are not possible, some rules of thumb can be supplied which will work in most cases. Probably the best measure of scatter is the Coefficient of Correlation mentioned above.

In the case of the overall regressions of profit versus sales, a correlation of less than + .90 should generally cause investigation. In analyzing detailed accounts, again, + .90 represents an effective lower limit of acceptance without investigation. In either case, a negative correlation should be an immediate red flag, since the negative sign indicates an upside-down or inverse relationship which should not exist in the set of cost-profit-volume relationships as a general rule.

In the case of Management Costs, a better measure is the degree of scatter around the mean or average value, expressed as a percentage of the average value. Use of the Standard Deviation as discussed in the following chapter would also be helpful. A range of plus or minus 10% might be acceptable. The causes for variation or scatter in excess of such a range should certainly be investigated.

A possible exception to this general rule may occur in investigating behavior in which some attempt has been made to distribute some type of fixed expense over varying sales volumes. This can cause an apparent inverse relationship. Such a situation should not occur if a proper and clear distinction is made between fixed and variable costs in detail.

3. UNCERTAINTY AND THE CURVE OF NORMAL DISTRIBUTION

The variation or "scatter" of individual data points around the average or trend line can be caused by seasonal variations, cyclical variations, a series of unpredictable random events, or by the operation of one or more of the causes for scatter mentioned in the previous chapter. In any case, the "scatter" is indicative of the degree of uncertainty which accompanies the statement of the average trend, even after all possible error sources have been eliminated and all reasonable corrections have been made.

In business, as well as in many natural phenomena, most variations are quite close to average, and decrease in frequency as the variation from average increases. Graphically, this is shown by the two curves in the following exhibit.

Both of these curves are "normal" curves in the sense that the greatest frequency of occurrence is near the middle or average, the frequency of occurrence drops off rapidly as the more extreme variations from average are approached, and the same frequency of occurrence exists on both sides of "average" so that the curves are symmetrical around the center line of "average"; that is, the right and left sides of the curves are mirror images of each other.

One will notice that, even at the extreme outer ends, the frequency of occurrence never quite reaches zero. This means that no matter how far the variation from average may be, there is always some chance, however slight, that it could happen.

The difference between these two curves is the extent of spread or "scatter." In one curve, scatter is limited, and most occurrences are clustered close to the average. In the other, "scatter" is much wider and the number of cases close to the average is smaller.

One cannot help asking how these two curves can be called normal

Exhibit 19

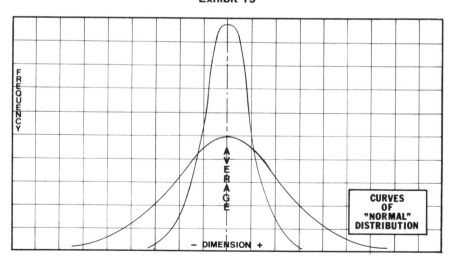

when they are different. The answer lies in use of a measure of disper-
sion or "scatter" which is called the Standard Deviation.

The Standard Deviation is the square root of the average squared
deviation (which is the sum of the squares of all the deviations from
average, divided by the number of cases as shown in the following
equation).

Standard Deviation

Where:

SD = Numerical Value of the Standard Deviation
 y = Actual cost or profit (vertical) for any sale (horiz)
 y' = Trend line value for same sale (x)
 N = Number of data points of x and y combinations

Equation 13: $SD = \sqrt{\dfrac{\text{Total of } (y - y')^2}{N}}$

If scatter is wide, the numerical value of the Standard Deviation will
be large. If scatter is small, the numerical value of the Standard Deviation will also be small. By dividing each individual deviation from average by the Standard Deviation, as shown in the following equation,
the deviations from average are expressed as a Standard Score in
Standard Deviation Units.

Standard Score

Where:

 z = Score in Standard Deviation Units
SD = Standard Deviation, as above
 D = $y - y'$ as above

Equation 14: $z = \dfrac{D}{SD}$

When so plotted, both curves, or any other "normal" curve will assume the truly normal form shown below. Note that the horizontal axis

is dimensioned in Standard Deviation Units, minus (− or negative) to the left of Average, and plus (+ or positive) to the right of Average.

The Normal Curve of Distribution as expressed in Standard Deviation Units also has an important relationship to probability which is shown in detail in the Appendix, **TABLE OF AREAS UNDER THE NORMAL CURVE.** This relationship becomes extremely useful in making quantitative appraisals of the chances of something happening or not happening in the future. Various applications will appear in later chapters.

In brief, however, as a illustration, the range from plus one (+1.00) Standard Deviation through average (0) to minus one (−1.00) Standard Deviation will include 68% of the possible occurrences, with 34% being above and 34% being below the average. The range from − 2.00 to + 2.00 Standard Deviations will include 95%, and from − 3.00 to + 3.00 will include 99%, etc. but the total will never quite reach 100%. Appendix 5, **TABLE OF AREAS UNDER THE NORMAL CURVE** shows the percentage probability of occurrence at various ranges of Standard Deviation Units from Average.

Since the Normal distribution is symmetrical about the Average, only the values for one side are shown in the TABLE. These must be doubled to show the entire range of probability from the minus side to the plus side.

Exhibit 20

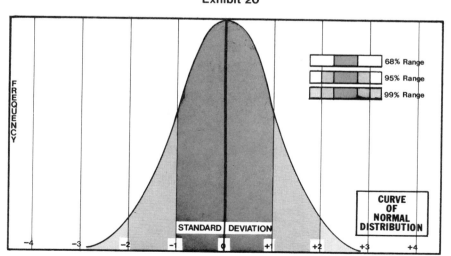

For example, the table shows a value of .3413 at 1.00 Standard Deviations (D/SD). This means that 34.13% of the probable cases will fall between Average and 1.00 Standard Deviation.

Doubling this value to show both plus and minus sides above and below Average would yield a value of 68.26% probability for the total range from − 1.00 SD to + 1.00 SD. Similarly, at 2.00 SD is the value .4773, or 47.73% between Average and 2.00 SD. Again, doubled, this gives a value of 95.43% for the entire range from − 2.00 SD to + 2.00 SD.

Our two companies, "A" and "B" from Chapter 2, Section 4, can now be compared as to risk. We have previously mentioned the "Margin of Safety," which is a direct expression of risk.

By calculating the Standard Deviation of the individual points from the trend line, we can establish the probability (based on this data), of the profits in some future period falling within some definite range around the profit path. We have done so for each company in the preceding exhibits, shading in a plus and minus one Standard Deviation band around the profit path of each company, giving a 68% probability of some future month falling within that band.

Notice how much wider the shaded band representing the 1 standard deviation range is in Exhibit 22 (Company B), as compared with Exhibit 21 (Company A). There is much more scatter present with Company B, and its range of uncertainty of prediction is much wider. As we saw in Section 2, there are several more or less valid reasons for such scattering, and the situation of the company demands detailed examination to find the particular source or sources of the scatter, and then to find means for eliminating those causes.

In Exhibit 10, we also showed average sales and profits for Companies A and B. This average profit is a direct indication of the margin of safety of the enterprise, since it is a direct measure of how much profits could decline before the enterprise begins to suffer a loss.

If we divide the average profits realized by each company by the corresponding value of the Standard Deviation for each company (which is plus or minus 91.19 monetary units for Company A and 3078.50 monetary units for Company B), we obtain the margin of safety in Standard Deviation Units. By looking for this value in the Table of Areas Under The Normal Curve (Appendix, Section 5) and adding 0.5 (to represent the complete other half of the curve of probability) we can determine the percentage of likelihood that the business

Exhibit 21

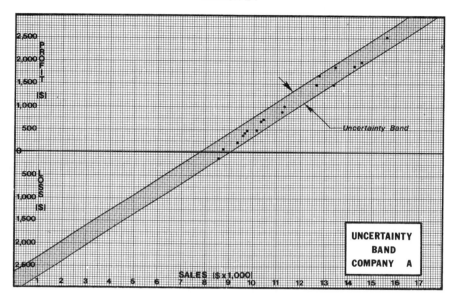

Exhibit 22

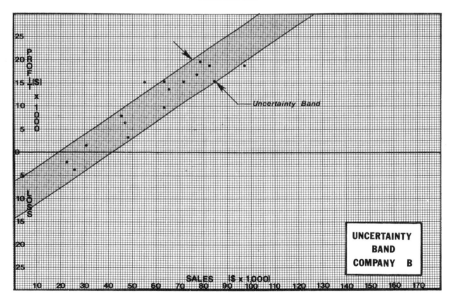

results in some future accounting period will show a profit. 1 minus the probability of profit (expressed as a decimal value) will, of course, show the probability of loss.

A comparison gage for our two sample companies is simply that of their respective margins of safety, expressed in standard deviation units, which places them on a common footing. The small Company A shows a margin of safety of:

Margins of Safety

Equation 15: $\dfrac{\text{Average Profit}}{\text{Standard Deviation}} = \dfrac{925}{91.19} = 10.14\ SD$

This means that Company A has a 99.99999 . . .% of continuing to show a profit.

Company B, while much larger, shows a much wider degree of scattering, and has a margin of safety of:

$$\frac{\text{Average Profit}}{\text{Standard Deviation}} = \frac{11{,}402}{3{,}078} = 3.70\ SD$$

This indicates a probability of 99.99% that Company B will continue to make a profit. A comparison indicates that Company A is in a somewhat safer position, by a ratio of 2.4 to 1. The example chosen here is, perhaps, not the best for both companies are sound. Small, new companies often show much higher scatter, and much lower margins of safety.

Consideration of the margin of safety and of the probabilities of loss or gain can, for example, be of great value in determining the credit worthiness of a company, either for a bank, or for the extension of commercial credit to a customer.

4. INTERPRETATION OF NEGATIVE INTERCEPTS

Occasionally, when using regression calculations to determine expense account behavior with variations in sales, one will find the trend line of a variable expense account passing through the horizontal axis and reaching the vertical axis on the negative side of the zero point.

If this "negative intercept" is at all substantial, it is a certain indication of the need for thorough investigation of the reporting and recording of that type of expense. This particular behavior is logically impossible under most circumstances. The logical implication of this behavior is that as sales decline, there is a point at which that specific expense not only ceases (where the trend line crosses the horizontal axis), but if sales decline further, cash actually begins to come into the company; an unlikely situation.

The negative intercept in the basic Profit Chart (Exhibit 6) which we have denoted as Management Costs is a special case. The implication here is of particular importance: it implies that the enterprise enters each accounting period in a *loss position by the amount of expected Management Costs for that period.*

This beginning loss position is gradually decreased throughout the accounting period by the accumulating Contribution from Sales at the rate of the Contribution Ratio in cents for each Dollar of Sales, until the loss position is paid off and Break-Even is attained.

After Break-Even has been attained, the entire Contribution from each additional dollar of Sales is pure pretax PROFIT.

Charts of *expense versus productive activity,* with productive activity as the independent variable, should *never* show a significant negative intercept. The appearance of a significant negative intercept is a certain indication of some error in bookkeeping or reporting.

When regression is used, particularly in the case of accounts showing considerable scatter, minor negative intercepts may appear, due to random happenings which interfere with the normal behavior. These might be ignored, but prudence indicates that they should be investigated.

5. PRODUCT VELOCITY, TURNOVER, AND HOLDING COSTS

The perfect business (as an ideal or a goal) is one with no requirements for working capital. In the ideal situation, goods come in, processing is done (with the help of the industrial engineer's ideal job), the finished goods are sold, paid for by the customer, and the supplier is paid, all in the same instant. Unfortunately, the real world is less than ideal.

When raw materials are purchased to begin production, or when goods are purchased for future sale, cost begins to accumulate. At the same time, this purchase ties up cash as soon as the material is paid for, thereby diminishing the liquidity of the enterprise. Yet income cannot be realized to replace the tied up cash until the finished items are *not only sold, but paid for by the customer.*

It is noteworthy that in a financial sense, the only difference between inventory and accounts receivable is that with inventory, the owner still has possession of the physical item, while in the case of an account receivable, he has given up possession of that material to the customer.

In either case, costs include the accumulated Management Costs during the processing or holding period, the interest cost on any money borrowed for working capital during this period, and, in the case of manufacturing, the conversion costs of raw material into finished goods. These costs often can be determined with some precision. In addition, there is yet another hidden cost which should receive consideration; the opportunity cost of the loss of use of the funds tied up in inventory and work in process.

It is generally accepted that cash in hand has more value than cash to come in at some time in the future. The further into the future the cash is due to come in, the less certain it is of coming in at all. At the same time, if that cash were in hand, it could possibly be invested elsewhere for more immediate profits, or, at least, the amount and cost of any borrowed money could be reduced.

Thus, a rental factor or progressive discount should apply to the value of inventory the longer it is held. The same consideration applies to Accounts Receivable.

In accord with normal investment practice, interest is not "simple," but compounds at some percentage rate for the duration of its application. Many of us see this happening with our savings accounts. These are moneys lent to the bank, and for which they pay rent or interest. If we do not withdraw this interest as earned, we, in fact, lend it back to the bank, and the bank is then obligated to pay more interest on the interest already earned. The compound interest equation is a simple one, but its workings are often not too well understood.

Compound Interest, Periodic Compounding

Where:

FV = Future value at the end of some time period.
PV = Present value or investment.
  i = Rate of interest, customarily expressed as a percent per year, and used in the formula as a decimal.
  a = Number of times per year compounding is done.
  N = Number of years.

Equation 16: $$FV = PV \left\{ 1 + \frac{i}{a} \right\}^{Na} = PV e^{iN}$$

For example, let us assume that we start a savings account with $100. The bank tells us that it will earn 6% per year, compounded quarterly. We plan to leave it with the bank for five years. We would like to know what our investment will be worth at the end of five years.

$$FV = 100 * \left\{ 1 + \frac{.06}{4} \right\}^{(4 * 5)} = 100 * 1.015^{20} = \$134.68$$

In the case of continuous compounding, the formula simplifies to the following.

Future Value, Continuous Compounding

Where:

e = 2.718281 . . . (the base of natural logarithms)

Equation 17: $FV = PV\, e^{iN}$

If our interest were to be compounded continuously, instead of quarterly, with the same rate of annual interest, our $100 investment would be worth:

$$FV = 100 * 2.718281\ldots^{(.06\,*\,5)} = 100 * 2.718281^{.30}$$
$$FV = \$134.99$$

In consideration of the progressive decline in value of payments of money to be received in the future as its return is progressively distant from the present, a similar set of principles must be employed, but in a discount fashion. This is seen in the following formula.

Present Value, Periodic Discounting

Equation 18:

$$PV = \frac{\dfrac{FV}{Na}}{\left\{1 + \dfrac{i}{a}\right\}}$$

For example, if we had a promise to receive $100 five years from now, and, again we were working with interest at 6% per year, compounded quarterly, and if we had a chance to sell that promise, what price should we ask in order to break even?

$$PV = \frac{100}{\left\{1 + \dfrac{.06}{4}\right\}^{(5\,*\,4)}} = \frac{100}{1.346855} = \$74.25$$

In the case of continuous compounding, the discount formula becomes the following.

Present Value, Continuous Discounting

Equation 19:

$$PV = \frac{FV}{e^{iN}}$$

In this case, the present value of our $100 would be:

$$PV = \frac{100}{1.3499} = 74.08$$

The Inventory Turnover ratio is an indicator of the liquidity of the inventory, or of the ease with which it could be converted into cash. The information comes from the Balance Sheet, and is another guidance ratio from that source. It is determined as follows.

Inventory Turnover Ratio

Where:

T = Number of times per year inventory is turned over
CG = Cost of Goods Sold
VI = Value of Average Inventory

Equation 20: $T = \dfrac{CG}{VI}$

From this ratio, a measure of the velocity of material though the enterprise can be developed as it passes through the enterprise from purchase to receipt of cash from the customer. This measure is derived by combining the Average Age of Inventory, calculated by Equation 21 below, with the Average Age of Accounts Receivable (from Chapter 4, Section 1).

Average Age of Inventory

Where:

AI = Average Age of Inventory

Equation 21: $AI = \dfrac{365}{T}$

Combining the Age of Inventory and the Age of Receivables yields the average length of time between receipt of material and receipt of payment. From this must be deducted the Average Age of Accounts

Payable, as determined from Equation 5. The result is the net time in which money is invested in inventory before it is returned by customer payments.

A minor error exists here, in that accounts payable occur for other reasons than purchase of inventory for eventual sale to customers. Supplies, utility bills, taxes, and a number of other things are also included. All of these items should properly be deducted from the total amount of accounts payable before determining the Age of Accounts Payable and from inventory for the purpose of determining the total time money is tied up in inventory.

The purchase cost of inventory then should be discounted at some annual interest rate (adjusted to reflect the Age of Accounts Payable) and the result deducted from the original purchase cost to determine the average holding cost of inventory. This, divided by the purchase cost of inventory, will yield the cost per dollar of average inventory holding cost. The resulting cost startles many people.

Most people in business fail to go through these calculations, and as a consequence, do not realize how important product velocity and inventory turnover can be in influencing both profit and cash flow. Accordingly, they fail to realize how much their profits could be improved by faster turnover or higher product velocity.

The next question is the annual interest rate to be used for compounding or discounting. At a minimum, it should be the rate being charged by banks for loans to businesses of similar risk. A case can be made for using the Contribution Ratio as a suitable interest rate, since this is the rate realized by the enterprise over and above the direct cost of production, and money tied up in work in process or inventory is not making any contribution to the Management Costs which continue during the holding period.

It is not necessary to do the complete present value calculations using the formulas listed above. These have been precalculated in the form of compound and discount Present Value Tables, shown in the Appendix. One merely selects the appropriate term in years, together with the rate of interest being used, and multiplies that by the amount of money under consideration.

In the case of fractional interest rates, an approximation may also be made by interpolating between the stated values, although the result will not be precise. If substantial sums are involved, it is better to apply the formula directly than to attempt to interpolate.

While the passage of time is continuous, and one would think that interest should compound in the same fashion, it should be noted that the continuously compounding formula is rarely used outside of the researcher. The closest approach to continuous compounding is made by those banks which compound daily.

In addition to the so-called interest tables, as seen in the Appendix, which may require interpolation or a considerable search for values for other than annual compounding, there are also a number of hand-held calculators now on the market, such as the Business Analyst made by Texas Instruments, which have the entire procedure built in. These produce results of high accuracy.

6. Analyzing the Operation

1. OPERATIONAL DIAGNOSIS

Our discussion to this point has been devoted almost entirely to the discovery of areas of needed attention and possible change in the operation of a business from the financial point of view. We have seen how sources of trouble can be located by these techniques. This has been given priority in presentation because the financial area is the crucial one, as well as the most likely avenue by which management can make discovery of existing or impending difficulty, and localize it. The financial approach by itself, however, is incomplete. Additional information is needed.

Earlier we discussed the manager as an agent for accomplishing changes. We can reaffirm this as a major function, but also we must enter some qualifications of this responsibility into the record.

When an unsatisfactory condition is found, real or potential, the concept of making changes becomes appropriate. However, changes cannot and must not be made blindly or indiscriminately. Making a change merely for the sake of creating something different can be deadly. If something is working, at least partially, it should not be changed until something better is developed.

It is particularly necessary for the exact nature of the problem to be clearly defined and delineated before any really effective changes can even be designed, let alone be implemented.

Having located a problem area through the preceding types of financial analysis and diagnosis, it becomes important to inquire why the problem exists, and what its real nature and configuration might be. Additional analytical and diagnositc techniques are necessary.

These techniques come mainly from the realm of industrial engineering, and consist essentially of an organized system and procedure of thought directed toward problem solving. The attitude basis on which this system of thought processes rests is one of **constant, but constructive dissatisfaction with things as they are.** Colloquially speaking, **"There MUST be a better way!"** Three principal steps are involved in making use of this type of thought process.

1. **ANALYSIS.** This step involves breaking the problem or process into its component parts for simplification and analysis in detail.

2. **EXAMINATION AND TEST.** In this step, each component is examined and tested to locate waste and unnecessary redundancies, using organized procedures which will be described in later paragraphs.

3. **SYNTHESIS.** This step involves reformulating the remaining components into new and more effective configurations, eliminating waste and unnecessary redundancy found in the preceding steps. This topic will be dealt with later in this chapter.

There are four inquiries which should be made about any segment of a business operation, any operational component, and about the business as a whole. We call them the four *Great Questions*. They should be asked repeatedly throughout the operation, even at the early step of establishing the basic goal of the enterprise. We will discuss each of the Questions separately in following sections.

The Great Questions

1. WHAT IS THE JOB?

2. WHAT SHOULD THE JOB BE?

3. HOW LONG DOES THE JOB TAKE?

4. HOW LONG SHOULD THE JOB TAKE?

By rigorous pursuit of the answers to these four questions, as we shall see, problems are discovered, dimensioned, and avenues toward solution are exposed.

2. THE JOB I

The first of the great questions to be asked in beginning an operational analysis of a business after gaining all the information possible from the financial data is:

"WHAT IS THE JOB?"

This has the look and sound of a tremendous oversimplification, which the reader may be tempted to dismiss lightly. Not so! Determination of what the organization or any segment of it really should be trying to accomplish is anything but an easy task.

To answer this question fully and properly often requires deep soul-searching on the part of management, as well as thorough probing of the organization. This question must be answered fully at all levels of the operation. To make things crystal clear and to secure unanimity of direction may require a searching review and restatement of the goals of the enterprise.

As was mentioned earlier, a well-defined goal, supported by a series of intermediate objectives and plans for implementation, is essential if the business is not to be a toy to be driven willy-nilly by any economic wind which might blow. Hard, sharply delineated quantitative answers are the proper avenue by which to avoid this fate.

In an ongoing business, top management rarely has the time available to comprehend every minute detail of the operation. Yet, if management is to manage capably and effectively, it must lay down clear paths for subordinates to follow, and these paths must be soundly determined. Consequently, it is almost impossible to avoid the need to have some member of top management be completely familiar with the problem area, even though a lower echelon employee may well have prepared the detailed analysis.

To determine the exact state of things is the first requisite in making effective improvements in the business. In so doing, it is most important to avoid any preconceptions or the making of any advance judgments, either of what is happening, or of what ought to be happening.

It is particularly important also to realize that the state of affairs which arouses the attention of management may only be a symptom; a sign of the existence of some malady as yet not defined or diagnosed.

Management has the option of merely treating the symptom, or attempting to eliminate the real source of the malady. In many cases, the choice may be between aspirin and surgery. A recent case may illuminate the process to be followed in making these analyses.

A client complained that serious discrepancies had occurred several times between the level of inventory as reported by the accounting records, and that disclosed by physical counts. These discrepancies had the repeated consistant effect of turning what was thought to be a tidy profit into an embarrassing loss.

A number of possible sources for these discrepancies were thought to exist:

1. Theft, by employees, or by others, perhaps with employee cooperation.
2. Not deducting stock issuances from the records.
3. Counting errors in putting away or issuing stock.
4. Clerical errors in arithmetic.
5. Overstatement of quantities by suppliers on incoming shipping documents, not verified by employees.

These error sources could have operated singly, or in various combinations. The problem was to determine precisely what the real causes were. A complete and detailed study was required of the exact procedures being followed in handling inventory transactions.

The procedure was to break the process into detailed component parts for study, then to study each component part, together with its inter-relationships to the other components. This analytical practice is hard to begin.

One often tends to overlook steps in the operation, or to pass them by without detailed analysis, and the more familiar one is with the operation, the more likely this is to happen. Intimate familiarity with an operation often leads to the expert making an assumption of knowledge on the part of a learner, trainee, or even an onlooker which that person really does not have.

Such oversights seriously interfere with effective training of employees, as well as cause the omission of important process steps or requirements. Actually, this careful, step-by-step process of analysis is the first key to the making of effective improvements.

In the case of clerical procedures and problems, or those of system design and operation, an appropriate instrument for seeing the sequence and relationship of these components is the flow chart, which lists each piece of paper or information in sequential steps, and shows their interconnections and inter-relationships. A sample flow chart is shown as Exhibit 23.

The value of the flow chart is that it presents this information in diagrammatic and pictorial form, which makes it much simpler to trace the process.

Exhibit 23 is actually the final revision incorporating corrective measures for the system errors found in this particular case. Use of such an instrument is also very helpful in visualizing and designing systems, and in training employees in using the system.

In the case under study, it was soon determined that the employees had no clear concept of what was required of them. It became clear that they were essentially honest, and that no theft was being attempted. Rather, they were simply somewhat confused human beings, who made mistakes.

What had not been realized by management was that the employees dealing with the various aspects of the inventory operation did not understand their individual detailed duties and responsibilities. Responsibility for the various procedural steps was diffused, job responsibilities were indistinct, and, as a result, errors were made and not corrected. There were no checks or balances.

Through a series of misunderstandings and errors, inventory was valued by means of a standardized gross profit rate, without regard to discounts given to customers. This resulted in inventory being overvalued on the books, and, because only a total monetary value was carried (instead of a record maintained by the number of pieces of each part on hand), the value of the pieces in inventory could never be matched with the inventory book value. The result was that management had deluded itself into a fool's paradise of expected profit, only to awaken to the shock of the real fact of loss.

In this case, as often happens, remedial measures were not what one would have expected from the beginning. The receiving system and some accounting procedures did need some minor redesign to correct procedural errors.

The principal avenue toward solution, however, lay in developing comprehensive written job descriptions of the duties and responsibilities of each employee, and then in conducting training sessions to as-

Exhibit 23

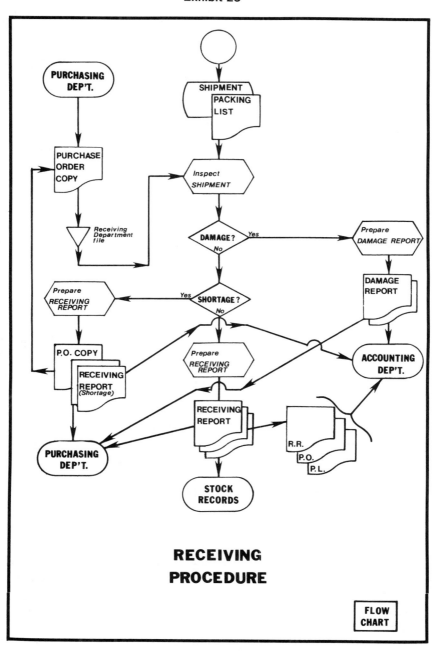

**RECEIVING
PROCEDURE**

sure that each employee understood his duties. (Refer to Chapter 12, Organization, Motivation, and Incentives for more detail.) From this point onward, it became the responsibility of management to see that each employee performed as required. In performing this step, organizational relationships, which had been confused at best, were clarified to the benefit of all involved.

A similar instrument for the study of manufacturing or other physical operations is the Flow-Process chart shown as Exhibit 24 below. This records the conversion process in detail, from raw material to a finished product.

In reviewing flow-process charts of manufacturing companies, there are three types of operations which should receive particular attention: Transport, Delay, and Store. The duration and distance moved are matters which should be recorded in detail, as these operations are particularly insidious sources of excessive cost.

The flow-process chart should record all of these accurately and fully for later analysis.

3. THE TIME I

The second Great Question still concerns the existing situation or the initial planning for new operations or products. It serves to add another essential dimension to the existing status. The question is:

"HOW LONG DOES THE JOB TAKE?"

The dimension of time required in relation to the work performed or to be performed is a matter of major concern to management. Management planning cannot be done without reference to time. Answering this question is essential to coordinating production, making delivery promises, and even in planning cash flow and financing. In addition, the time dimension can become quite important in evaluating various operations and costs.

Earlier we saw that knowledge of the past is our only stepping stone

Exhibit 24

FLOW PROCESS CHART   Page ___ of ___

PART NUMBER_____

PART NAME_____

PROCESS_____

DEPARTMENT_____

OBSERVER _____ DATE _____

	SUMMARY	No.
○	OPERATIONS	
⇨	TRANSPORTS	
☐	INSPECTIONS	
D	DELAYS	
▽	STORAGES	
	TOTAL STEPS	
	DISTANCE MOVED	

STEP	Operation Transport Inspect Delay Storage	DESCRIPTION OF ☐ PRESENT ☐ PROPOSED METHOD
	○⇨☐D▽	
	○⇨☐D▽	
	○⇨☐D▽	
	○⇨☐D▽	
	○⇨☐D▽	
	○⇨☐D▽	
	○⇨☐D▽	
	○⇨☐D▽	
	○⇨☐D▽	
	○⇨☐D▽	
	○⇨☐D▽	
	○⇨☐D▽	
	○⇨☐D▽	
	○⇨☐D▽	
	○⇨☐D▽	
	○⇨☐D▽	
	○⇨☐D▽	
	○⇨☐D▽	
	○⇨☐D▽	
	○⇨☐D▽	
	○⇨☐D▽	
	○⇨☐D▽	

to the future. We have also seen the need to have this knowledge in quantitative terms.

Historically, Frederick Taylor, working in the U.S.A. in the early twentieth century was the first to attack the problem of adding the dimension of time to the production problem in an organized fashion. Even today, his methods are still in use in many locations throughout the world, and are still proving to be useful and adequate in many cases.

He pioneered the concept of breaking the job into its constituant parts (operations), and these operations into smaller components which he, and we today, label elements. (In his time, the chemical element was thought to be the ultimate subdivision of matter, so he conceived the "element" as the fundamental minimum unit of work.) He was also responsible for the use of the stopwatch to measure elemental times with precision.

As technology evolved, production requirements became higher, and the volume of mass production grew. Consequently, workers' jobs became more and more refined and specific, and, because of simplification, increased in the pace of motions and the amount of repetitive motion. The combination of fast pace and repetitive high volume production caused smaller and smaller improvements and savings to become economically significant. The result was that the stopwatch was no longer adequate to measure these operations.

Higher speed measuring and recording devices were required, including motion pictures which preserved a visual record of the operation in minute detail and could be studied at leisure.

In more recent time, production pressures and the extent of high-volume repetition have increased to the point of making even minute improvements economically worthwhile.

In this process, as in the translation from chemical to atomic knowledge and technology, a finer subdivision of the work element was required; the micromotion.

The late H. B. Maynard of Pittsburgh, Pennsylvania was and is perhaps the best known researcher into the measurement and standardization of micromotion. His Methods-Time-Measurement (MTM) system has been widely adopted throughout the world.

The stopwatch is, however, still a very useful tool for measuring many operations in which it presents an adequate level of refinement. Exhibits 25 and 26 show a form used to organize the information

Exhibit 25

STUDY NO. DATE **TIMESTUDY OBSERVATION SHEET** SHEET OF

NO.	ELEMENT DESCRIPTION	T	W	T	W	T	W	T	W	T	W	T	W	T	W	T	W	T	W	T	W	T	W	T	W	T	W	T	W	T	W

FOREIGN ELEMENTS			
S	T	W	DESCRIPTION
A			
B			
C			
D			
E			
F			
G			
H			
J			
K			
L			
M			
N			

LEVELING

SKILL		EFFORT	
+.15	Super	+.12	Excessive
+.10	Excellent	+.08	Excellent
+.05	Good	+.04	Good
.00	Average	.00	Average
-.10	Fair	-.07	Fair
-.20	Poor	-.15	Poor

CONDITIONS		CONSISTENCY	
+.06	Ideal	+.04	Perfect
+.04	Excellent	+.02	Excellent
+.02	Good	+.01	Good
.00	Average	.00	Average
-.03	Fair	-.02	Fair
-.07	Poor	-.04	Poor

SUMMARY

ELEMENT NUMBER	1	2	3	4	5	6	7	8	9	10	11	12	13	14	15	16	17
Total Time																	
Number of Observations																	
Average Time																	
Minimum Time																	
Maximum Time																	
Net Leveling Factor																	
Leveled Time																	
P. F. & S. Allowance																	
Allowed Time																	

NET	SKILL	EFFORT	COND.	CONSIST.

START	FINISH	ELAPSED

ROBERT N. HOGSETT

TS 1 A-66

Exhibit 26

TIMESTUDY OBSERVATION SHEET

DEPARTMENT	OPERATION		PART DESCRIPTION
OPERATOR	CLOCK NUMBER	DRAWING NUMBER	
		MOULD	DIE	STYLE	ITEM
MACHINE		PATTERN	QUALITY SPEC	MATERIAL

EL NO	ELEMENT DESCRIPTION		Small Tool Nos, Speed, Depth of cut, Etc.	Feed, Note	Speed Tool Life,	Element Allowed Time	Foreign Element Allowed Time Per Cycle	Total Element Allowed Time

SPECIAL TOOLS, JIGS, FIXTURES, ETC

CONDITIONS

OBSERVER	APPROVED	DATE

Setup Allowance	Pcs/Setup	Pcs/Setup	Setup/Pc:	TOTAL

REMARKS

ROBERT R. HODGETT

TS 10-66

derived from stopwatch studies. It requires detailed information and sets forth the complete story of the particular job under study.

Notice that to complete this form fully and properly requires not only recording a full description of the operational elements, interferences, delays, and other factors, but information as to tooling, equipment, and workplace layout as well.

The application of work measurement has now been successfully applied to almost all aspects of productive work, both factory and office. However, clocking is not the only way of accomplishing this result. There are many types of jobs which are relatively nonrepetitive in nature. Many maintenance, indirect labor, office, clerical, and lower and middle management jobs fall into this category.

Measurement of these types of work is also desirable, yet they are difficult and uneconomical to measure by conventional stopwatch methods. Statistical methods, generally classified under the heading of "Work Sampling" have been developed to deal with the problem of obtaining measurements of these types of operation economically.

In applying this technique, many random observations are taken of employees, and records are maintained as to the particular activity being engaged in at the time of observation. The frequency with which a particular activity occurs has been shown to relate directly to the proportion of the employee's time devoted to that activity.

All that is needed is a sufficient number of observations to make a statistically reliable sample (Sample sizes for acceptable levels of accuracy are shown in Section 2 of Chapter 13). From these observations, the frequency of occurrence of each item is in direct proportion to the portion of the employee's time devoted to this activity.

These techniques of job break-down and measurement can be applied to every aspect of business operation. Direct and indirect labor clerical, sales, and even janitorial operations can benefit from this type of analysis.

Determination of a measured, quantitative answer to the question "How long does the job take?" is very important as a basis for later selection and evaluation of alternatives, for costing, and for planning. Without it, management is missing a vital dimension with which to view its duties.

Also, without a quantitative statement as to time requirements, many of the other improved techniques for management, planning, and operation could not be applied.

7. Examination and Test

1. SEARCH FOR THE BETTER WAY

In the preceding chapter, we answered the first two great questions, "WHAT IS THE JOB?" and "HOW LONG DOES THE JOB TAKE?" and we established the necessary historical basis from which to plan the future. We are now in position to analyze the present situation to see if this is as it should be, or whether **"THERE IS A BETTER WAY."**

Here we enter the realm of the methods engineer, the systems designer, and the tool and manufacturing engineer. Yet, as specialized as these occupations may seem to be, top management itself can put the same type of thinking to effective use.

Again, as has been said several times earlier, the basic attitude should be one of **CONSTRUCTIVE DISSATISFACTION.**

The thought process consists of a detailed examination and inquiry into each operation and each operational element, questioning all aspects, and even its need to exist at all. Some of the questions which should be asked are listed below as a sort of checklist to assure that each step is thoroughly explored.

In pursuing this procedure, it is important to question everything. As we shall see in Chapter 10, Section 4 on Zero Base Budgeting, it is vital to question everything, and to avoid the trap of accepting anything because it has previously existed.

1. What is the objective?
2. What does this step propose to accomplish?
3. Does this step advance the process?
4. Is there some necessary step which has been omitted?
5. Is this step really necessary?
6. Why?

7. What would happen if it were to be eliminated?
8. If this step is truly necessary, is this the only way of accomplishing it?
9. Are there other, faster, cheaper, more accurate ways?
10. Is there another point in the sequence of operations at which this step could be better and more effectively accomplished?
11. Can this step be combined with another, so that the combination becomes more effective?
12. Is the workplace properly laid out so the worker's efforts are used efficiently?

This list of inquiries is not complete. There are many others which a good analyst will generate in order to thoroughly test each operation of the existing situation or plan.

In making the above type of inquiry, an opportunity also occurs to judge the contributions, knowledge, and understanding of any employees who might be involved in carrying out the process under study.

On the Flow-Process chart (Exhibit 24) the arrow symbol indicating a move or transport operation is needful of special attention whenever it occurs. Material handling is one of the most costly and wasteful aspects of manufacturing, and of many other types of enterprise. It has a tendency to increase constantly unless given special and continuing attention.

It must constantly be kept in mind that *to move something creates immediate cost,* and, unless in making that move something is done which advances the product toward completion, the result is an increase in cost without a corresponding increase in value created. Very often, material handling will consume half or more of the total cost of production.

There is one exception to this at times, in that there is utility value in transporting something from where it exists to where it is needed, such as taking ore to a smelter. However, even this aspect should be questioned to assure it is needed.

Even in an established, ongoing production situation, continued monitoring of material handling methods and costs is essential. Workers themselves are not usually conscious of the cost of material handling, and will often introduce extra handling steps unwittingly, as they will also change the methods of operation.

The operations of "Storage" and "Delay" also need special attention.

As we mentioned previously, these represent additions to cost, and tend to decrease both liquidity and profit.

The operation of "Inspection" can cause trouble. The drives for production volume, and for the maintenance of product quality are often in direct opposition to each other. Too much attention to quality control can lead to excessive cost, while too little can lead to loss of sales, and consequent loss of profit. The check list of questions can be fully applied to quality control operations as well as all the others.

More important than merely following a check list is the thought principal and attitude on the part of the analyst. The attitude of **"CONSTRUCTIVE DISSATISFACTION"** is the start, coupled with a hard-working imagination to envision the various possible recombinations of work elements which would get the required job done in a simpler and less costly manner. A good methods person examines and tests sequences, relationships, and needs. He runs them backward, inside out, and upside-down, all the while questioning **WHY, WHY, WHERE, HOW,** and, foremost, **IS THIS REALLY NECESSARY?**

At times, of course, real technological breakthroughs in methods are achieved by inspired strokes of sheer genius, without any particular background of sequential thought. Yet geniuses are few and far between, and we cannot always expect them to produce on any sort of a schedule. Consequently, the remainder of us nongenius types must depend upon attitude, perseverence, and a check list of sorts. By rigorous examination of need, and by exercise of imagination to develop alternatives, even we nongeniuses can achieve substantial improvements.

A similar mode of thought was discussed in Chapter 2, Section 4, making use of brainstorming to develop different scenarioes and possibilities. We denoted this as playing the game of "What If?"

As applied to work methods, such a free-flowing type of idea generation, tracing out the causes why something cannot be done in a certain manner can often lead to highly effective innovations of an unsuspected type or nature, perhaps existing at some apparent distance from the original problem, yet exercising a profound effect on it. Only a free and unfettered imagination will accomplish this. Yet more of us ordinary types than one would ever expect can accomplish great strides by casting aside all inhibitions to our imagination, refusing to discard any idea whatsoever without full test, and really **THINKING.**

We all labor under the load of tradition. The urge to follow established paths can often inhibit our ability to think freely and to imagine boldly to a far greater extent than we would care to admit.

This was evident to the author on a recent trip to India to lecture on this very subject. With four thousand years of recorded history upon their shoulders, its people are struggling to modernize, and to adopt the technology of the Western World, in the face of a tradition of manual labor, tremendous numbers of people, and a relative scarcity of raw materials, particularly as compared with the United States.

In attempting practice cases in methods improvement with Indian students of industrial engineering, and even in discussion with senior executives of Indian enterprises, there was a very frequently evidenced tendency to stop short of full pursuit of the best available method; a tendency to be inhibited in imagining all the way to an ultimate possibility. Almost always, there was failure to appreciate the true value of human effort as a scarce and precious asset. Yet material resources were valued highly.

Such a situation naturally interferes with their ability to adopt Western technology in a truly effective fashion, for Western development, particularly in the United States, has sprung from a plethora of natural resources, coupled with a real scarcity of human labor, leading naturally to the underlying concept that the labor of a human being is a resource of great value, to be expended only with the greatest prudence and care.

This fundamental concept, in the opinion of the author, is largely responsible for the development of the capital-intensive, highly productive economy and culture of the Western countries.

The attitude of CONSTRUCTIVE DISSATISFACTION, persistently and resolutely maintained is the key to progress.

8. Techniques of Synthesis

1. MAKING OPERATIONAL IMPROVEMENTS

In planning the manufacture of a new item or product, the same type of analytical break-down as previously discussed in developing flow and flow-process charts becomes necessary. In addition, when planning has been completed, an instrument is needed to record the planning, and to issue the appropriate instructions to manufacturing personnel.

Initial input for this planning is, of course, the engineering information as to specifications and configurations of parts and assemblies, which should absolutely and completely describe the product. From this information, production planning can begin.

In the manufacture of any product, there are usually a series of distinct steps or operations involved, each of which requires analysis, study, and planning for proper completion. Failure to work out manufacturing details with sufficient care and accuracy has led to the eventual downfall of many manufacturing enterprises.

Many craftsmen can and do work out the required manufacturing steps in their heads without committing them to paper. In some cases of simple and nonrepetitive work, this is all that is necessary. In most cases, however, such procedure results in sub-optimal operation and waste of time, material, and energy through incomplete or absent planning or unforeseen events. If a sustained manufacturing effort is contemplated, it is far better to proceed by way of the formal, written planning mode.

The vehicle normally used in formulating and recording manufacturing procedures is the Operation Sheet, one type of which is shown below as Exhibit 27. This form provides appropriate spaces for the listing of all pertinent information concerning the particular part, each operation to be performed, machines, equipment, tooling, etc. Data

Exhibit 27

OPERATION SHEET
DETAIL PARTS

PART NO. _____ ISSUE DATE _____

NAME_____ DWG. NO. _____PCS. REQ. _____

MATERIAL _____CONDITION_____

NEXT ASSEM. _____ PCS/ASSEM. _____

OPER. NO.		DEPT	MACH.	TOOLS	STD. TIME / PC.	DUE OUT

from the Operation Sheet is often combined with the making of a Flow-Process chart to assure that there is the minimum of wasted time and effort.

Having precisely determined the existing situation by means of studies, flow charts, or flow-process charts, or having established a first-time sequence of operations for a new product, item, or service, we can enter the second phase of the three-step process, that of evaluation.

It should be noted here that this process cannot just be done once and then forgotten. Most progress is indeed evolutionary in nature. Consequently, management is and will be required as a condition of survival to undertake a continuous process of self re-evaluation along the foregoing lines.

Knowledge is continually increasing. New and improved machines and tools are continually being built. Competition and technological advances keep things in a continual state of flux and evolution. Further, humans do not always see their way to optimum solutions on the first trial, or even on the tenth. As we have seen, some potential exists for continued improvement until the ideal of the industrial engineer is realized, and wealth is created at no cost and with no labor or time consumed.

In the U.S.A. and elsewhere, we have a phenomenon which we label "creeping change" which is both a curse and a blessing. Regardless of how we may choose to view it, it does represent a real and continuing problem requiring the constant attention of management.

Creeping change is usually created by the individual worker, who develops his own way of doing his particular job, instead of sticking to the specified method. Many times, this is a real improvement and should be adopted generally. At other times it is harmful, sometimes resulting in quality decline, increased cost, or, in some cases, actual product failure.

If a product and its operational plan and tooling have been well planned, one could well question why there should be any possibility for improvement. The answer is that we are imperfect human beings, and what we may consider to be the "one best way" today can well be completely overturned by someone's more penetrating and thorough thought tomorrow.

It is quite possible that if you were to take a walk through any factory, you could recommend some immediate improvements. It is equally possible that I, following in your footsteps, could improve upon your work, that you, in turn, could still improve on mine, and so on . . . a never-ending process.

Continuous care also must be exercised to see that improvements are placed into operation and so maintained. If employees are not properly instructed, trained, and supervised in maintaining performance, creeping change will certainly begin sooner than would otherwise be the case, or management will not receive the full benefit of the time and effort spent on making improvements.

The important thing to consider here is that the need for and possibility of improvement is never ending, and that without continuing attention by management, it will not occur except for what creeping changes may be introduced by the workers themselves. Instead, through complacency, decline becomes probable.

The point to remember is that change will occur, and most times it is better that changes are planned, controlled, and tested, rather than just "happening."

In summary, the most important things are three in number:

1. To break down the process into small steps, each of which can easily be understood, examined, and dealt with.

2. To examine rigorously the need for and placement of each single step.

3. To permit nothing to be done in any productive process which has not been proved to be essential to produce the required results.

By following these principles, and maintaining a constant attitude of **CONSTRUCTIVE DISSATISFACTION** with the present state of things, the enterprise should be in a constant state of evolutionary improvement, and increasing profit.

2. THE JOB II

We should return to the checklist of questions given in Chapter 1, Section 7, and in a step-at-a-time, methodical way, review each and every operational element, and each and every operation, to assure that:

1. No production operation or operation element is performed until proven essential.

2. Time and human effort devoted to production operations and operation elements is minimized.

3. No transport, delay, inspection, storage, or operation is performed or permitted unless absolutely necessary, so that maximum product velocity is maintained.

4. The flow of work is straightforward, with the minimum of backtracking and potential or real interferences.

5. Material handling labor is minimized, and automated to the maximum practical extent.

6. Human effort used in performing the various operations is minimized, and used only when it is the best or only way of performing the operation.

7. Movement of material and information through the operational processes is as rapid as possible consistent with maintaining the required level of quality.

By maintaining constant pressure toward continually discovering and making improvements, management has the best chance to remain competitive, to improve its competitive position, and to improve profits.

Having done so, the great question **"WHAT SHOULD THE JOB BE?"** can be considered to have been answered, *TEMPORARILY!*

3. THE TIME II

The last great question can only be asked after the job has been optimized and clearly established. That question is:

"HOW LONG SHOULD THE JOB TAKE?"

What should be expected of an average employee is indeed a thorny question. Now we are at the point of establishing standards against which actual performance can be measured. The idea of having a standard is no different from having any other planned situation, which is then to be controlled through the operation of the feedback principle.

Always, when people are required to perform work, there is a question of "How fast?" This is a legitimate question. The answer is important to management for a number of reasons, not the least of which is that of needing to make sound delivery promises to customers.

In concept, the idea of a standard for performance is easy to come to, and the need is well demonstrated. However, achieving a workable, realistic standard for job performance is, even today, highly controversial in some quarters. We shall discuss some ways of arriving at standards, which, although less than perfect, have proved to be workable.

The first thing to remember is that a standard for performance, to be effective and valid, must be based on a very specific way of doing the job. This method, together with the supporting tooling, equipment, forms, files, etc., should be carefully established by means of the previously discussed analytical methods we saw in answering the previous great question "WHAT SHOULD THE JOB BE?"

The answer to the preceding question should always be clearly, carefully, and thoroughly documented. If there should be any change in the product, workplace arrangement, material, tools, or equipment, any previously established standard is *immediately invalidated.* The job should be restudied, and a new standard established.

To establish standards, there must be some agreed and easily tested understandings, in quantitative form, as to what "normal" or base performance is.

Performance is usually expressed as some form of work pace. Normal Performance has been generally defined in subjective terms as follows.

Normal Pace is that pace which an experienced worker can maintain throughout the work day without unreasonable fatigue.

Through extensive research, several base points for "normal" or standard performance have been established. Among these are walking at a pace of 3 miles per hour (264 feet per minute, 80.47 meters per minute, or with a military 30-inch or 762-cm pace, 106 paces per minute).

For hand motions, the base would be a pace such as would deal a pack of fifty-two playing cards into four piles at the corners of a one-foot square, dealing single cards in a clockwise pattern in one minute.

With norms such as this, movies showing workers operating the same process at different rates of speed have been prepared for training of timestudy observers. The expectation is that the observer will judge the pace of a worker under observation in comparison with their memory of the pace films, and adjust the time allowance to "normal." It is customary in a well run operation for timestudy observers to undergo constant training in pace rating so as to retain consistency.

This may seem to be an unusually subjective way of arriving at an objective result, but it has been well demonstrated that observers can be so trained and can make sound and consistent ratings within an acceptable range of variances.

There are some more refined ways of rating the worker for the purposes of leveling observed times to "normal." In the lower right-hand corner of the sample timestudy form, Exhibit 26, there is a special section for leveling the observed performance. This takes into account several different aspects of worker performance, and has been arrived at by substantial field testing. Use of the rating factors tends to ease the problem of leveling and make its application more consistent.

If there is high repetition and much employee specialization, it is more prudent to make use of some form of predetermined motion times, such as Methods-Time-Measurement, previously mentioned.

In any event, a note of caution should be sounded. Cost versus benefits should always be a major consideration. Making the foregoing analyses will always involve cost. Consequently one should never spend more to make a study than one can reasonably expect to realize in improvements from its results. We will discuss methods of evaluation in later sections.

9. Production and Inventory Planning and Control

1. PLANNING; CPM AND PERT

Often we have spoken of the need for various types of planning. In previous chapters we discussed operational planning through the use of flow charts and flow-process charts. Unless summarized, in some fashion, it becomes quite difficult to make any sort of prediction as to when something will be completed.

Yet we must continually make such predictions for many purposes. In manufacturing, we must schedule work through the various operations. To get orders or contracts, we often must bind ourselves to fixed delivery dates or schedules. Therefore, answering the fourth great question of the previous chapter, "HOW LONG SHOULD THE JOB TAKE?" becomes of vital importance.

The first step, in the case of a manufactured product, or a process is to prepare a product tree or explosion of the successive operations and/or parts in succession from finished product to raw material. Colloquially, this may be termed a "Goes-into" chart. A sample is shown below as Exhibit 28.

Unfortunately, such a chart only tells what assembles to which and in what order. It says nothing about how long anything will take to complete. Further, it says nothing really sound about reporting progress toward completion.

The first step in this direction was the invention of a new chart form by Henry Gantt. The Gantt chart supplies a method of recording in summary form the progress made each day, week, or month on each part, order, or product. A typical Gantt chart appears below as Exhibit 29.

Unfortunately, the Gantt chart, despite its many ingenious applica-

Exhibit 28

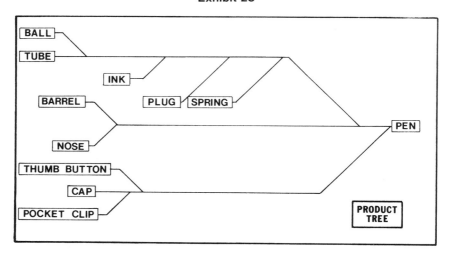

tions cannot distinguish which operational sequences are critical to the determination of how long a project will take. It cannot deal with potential interferences, or competition among various parts for use of the same machinery or floor space. In a complex product, such as an airplane, this can become a very serious drawback.

In the later stages of World War II, when the demand for aircraft and similar complex machines was particularly severe, an improved method for dealing with the problem of complex scheduling was evolved called the "Critical Path Method" or "CPM."

In applying this method, one works along the product tree, and its subsidiary operational breakdowns to determine what order of precedence or sequences of operations and parts manufacture and assembly are essential to make the end product in its finished state. Each part, assembly, or operation will have a beginning point and an ending point. These points are labeled events.

The ruling question is:

Exhibit 29

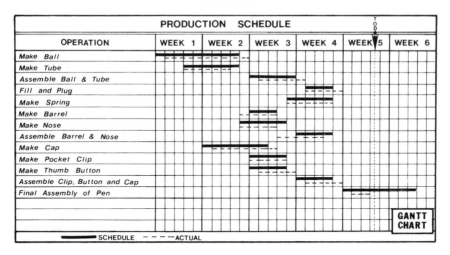

WHAT PARTS AND/OR OPERATIONS MUST BE COM-
PLETED BEFORE THIS ONE CAN BEGIN?

The starting and ending events for each operation, part, or assembly
are separated by a span of time. From the exercise of imagination and
planning, there are certain sequences or orders of precedence which
must exist or be established. We know from this, for example, that the
starting event of item B cannot occur until after the ending event of
item A. A great deal of this is worked out in the writing of Assembly
Operation Sheets by manufacturing engineers and planners.

The event sequence which will determine the completion time for
the product or project is the mandatory sequence or chain of connected
events reaching from start to finish which requires the greatest total
time span. This is the "Critical Path." All other event chains can be
completed inside of this total time span.

It is vital here that there be reasonable estimates as to the time
needed to complete each step. Failing this, prediction of completion
dates is impossible. Standards for labor performance are particularly
valuable for this purpose.

The timing of the start and finish of noncritical event chains can be
determined in the same manner as the Critical Path for the Project.
That is, their individual critical paths must be worked backward from

the required completion event which must precede entry to the main path. From this, starting times for these subsidiary event chains can be determined.

In a complex product or project, there may be several successive levels of event chains below the Critical Path, each one representing the critical path for subsidiary event chains. Exhibit 30 below shows a simplified diagram of the critical path for a product.

In a manufactured product, or the rendering of a standardized service, analysis of the critical path need only be done once, unless methods and tooling changes are developed, and then redone only a few times. The various forms of contracting pose a different problem. With a contractor, most times each job undertaken is new and different, with enough changes so that previously established methods and time sequences will not be applicable. Such a person then must erect a new plan for each project.

Even though this can become quite laborious, the savings in overall time and cost for a project with any serious degree of complexity more

Exhibit 30

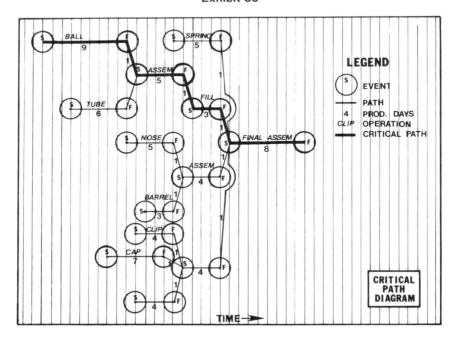

than makes up for the planning labor. Management is able to concentrate on making the critical path dates, with some degree of confidence that if the timing required for the critical path is maintained, the minor items will fall into place and the project will be finished on time.

The construction industry is one which has in recent years made extensive and worthwhile use of critical path planning.

Subsequently, a further advance was made by the introduction of the Program Evaluation and Review Technique, known as PERT. This technique recognizes the uncertainty of meeting specific future completion dates due to the intrusion of unknown outside, possibly random, events or accidents.

This is done by the introduction of not one but three time spans between events: an optimistic value ("Oh, it can't possibly be done before ————"); a probable value ("It will probably take about ————, so it should be finished by ————"); and a pessimistic value, ("Oh, it certainly should take no more than ————, no matter what happens, unless the world comes to an end").

The earliest completion date for the project would be determined by the critical path involving only the optimistic estimates. The latest date would be the critical path involving only the pessimistic estimates, and the probable would be the critical path involving only the probable estimates.

By running the critical paths of the combinations and permutations of the three types of estimates, a probability distribution can be developed by which probability ranges of completion dates can be calculated, using the Table of Areas Under the Normal Curve.

In using PERT, however, the principles of feedback looping are applied. Progress on the project is continuously monitored, and probabilities are recalculated based on results to date. In this manner, it becomes possible to locate and act on delays along the critical path, without diverting attention to noncritical matters.

Although PERT has proved its value on many projects, including vehicles and support for the historic journeys to the moon, several cases of apparent failure have been noticed in recent years, notable among which are the many delays encountered in the space shuttle program.

The reason for this particular apparent failure is fairly obvious. The space shuttle program is working on the very outer fringes of present technological knowledge, with many more unknowns than usual. The result has been that the time estimates were inadequate for the types of glitches which occurred. The failures were a result of human error, rather then of the system itself.

Applications of CPM and PERT are helpful not only in coordinating and controlling the physical conduct of a project, but also can be very important in planning the financial aspects, both as to income flow, and requirements for borrowing. Since borrowing involves interest cost, it is unwise to borrow sooner than needed, under penalty of paying more interest than necessary.

Manual tracing of all the possible permutations and combinations of event chains can become very cumbersome and time-consuming in the case of a complex product. Hence, to operate PERT successfully usually will require use of a computer to handle all the mathematical repetitions with reasonable speed. In many cases, the program for doing so would require special development.

The increasing availability of microcomputers to managers of small businesses is gradually placing these techniques within their financial reach, although development of personal programming competence to bring the cost of special programs within reach is still a problem.

2. ESSENTIALS OF INVENTORY PLANNING AND CONTROL

As was mentioned in an earlier chapter, the ideal business transaction is one in which the dealer buys or makes the merchandise, the customer takes the merchandise, pays for it immediately, and the dealer takes his profit and pays the supplier, all in the same instant of time. Since this is not possible, we must work with a less than ideal situation.

This demands either delaying delivery to the customer until the merchandise is received, or carrying inventory of some sort. Most business people choose to carry inventory for several good reasons.

1. In the case of items usually bought on impulse or for immediate consumption, if the customer cannot obtain immediate delivery, he will go elsewhere. This represents a lost sale.

2. In the case of a manufactured item, rarely does the manufacturer control the source of his various raw materials or purchased parts. To protect himself against delayed shipments from suppliers, he carries an inventory of raw materials and purchased parts.

3. In many cases, customers will not buy an item sight unseen. In such case, if the merchant is to make a sale, he must have sufficient stock for the customer to see and from which to select. This is particularly true in the case of big ticket items, such as furniture, televisions, autos, and the like. It is also noticeable in such items as shoes and clothing, where the same item and style is offered in several sizes or configurations.

As was mentioned earlier in Chapter 5, Section 5 on Product Velocity, Turnover, and Holding Cost, buying inventory locks up cash which cannot be used for other purposes until the merchandise is not only sold, but paid for. Financing inventory is a major problem for many businesses. The purpose of inventory control is to assure that, to the greatest practical extent, what is needed is on hand when needed (for production or sale), while at the same time locking up no more cash in inventory than is absolutely essential to accomplish this purpose.

The first major problem for many small businesses is that of establishing and maintaining the necessary records of purchases, deliveries, usage by period, and cost by which inventory management can be fine tuned. Without attempting any refinement, even keeping a ready reference record of what is on hand can be costly and extremely burdensome in some cases.

One of the author's clients, a retail auto parts store, lists over 15,000 different items in its inventory, with an office force of one full-time and one part-time person to do all the record keeping. The many rapid price changes for their inventory items have posed an almost impossible burden to maintain the records with any degree of accuracy. Nonetheless, this must be done, lest the cost of holding inventory become uncontrollable.

The holding cost of inventory must include the cost of the paperwork of ordering, recording, and dispensing as well as material-handling labor, insurance, heating and cooling, the cost of storage space, and all the other little items often forgotten but which eat up money because of the decision or need to carry inventory. To this must be added the complication of quantity discounts by suppliers. There is a distinct and determinable cost connected with the preparation of any piece of paperwork, whether it be a letter, a purchase order, or whatever. In the case of a purchase order, for example, as with the other costs of order entry, this cost is independent from the quantity or unit cost of the item being ordered.

The cost of order preparation, order control, receiving, and the like, coupled with the cost of holding inventory and with whatever quantity discounts may be offered makes necessary consideration of what the correct and economical ordering and stocking quantity should be. Specialists and stock control people talk glibly about EOQ much to the mystification of the remainder of us mortals.

EOQ is simply shorthand for **Economical Ordering Quantity;** that quantity to order which will provide the appropriate availability to customers at the minimum unit cost. Determination and use of Economic Ordering Quantities is always important, but is of particularly great importance at the time of writing this work because of the high rate of inflation, the high cost of money, and the looming possibility of a severe economic downturn.

Two principal factors interact in determining the size of the EOQ; the cost of getting the item into possession, and the cost of holding it until sold. We have discussed the problems and need for determining inventory holding cost previously. We have not yet discussed the cost of getting the item into our possession. Another consideration is the time needed to replace an item sold; the replacement lead time.

These costs include such things as order-writing cost, incoming freight charges, receiving and stocking costs, excess charges for buying quantities less than that offering the greatest price discount, and a lot of other things, small in themselves, but combining to make up a substantial item of cost.

Affecting the total of inventory holding cost is the quantity ordered and held in inventory, as compared with the rate of withdrawal or sale from that inventory. This can be determined by reference to the average age of inventory as discussed in early chapters. With a given rate of usage or withdrawal, the average age of inventory will grow as the quantity ordered increases. EOQ can be determined by applying the following formula.

Economical Ordering Quantity

Where:

EOQ = Economical Ordering Quantity
U = Usage; number of pieces used per year
C = Cost per piece
O = Ordering cost (including set-up in manufacturing)
H = Rate of annual Holding Cost (Percent)

Equation 22: $EOQ = \sqrt{\dfrac{2UO}{HC}}$

The result of an application of this formula can be seen in the following graph.

Some of these quantities may be a little difficult to determine, and

Exhibit 31

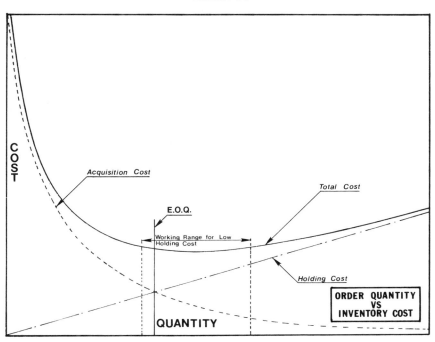

application of the formula will take some work if applied to every item in, for example, an auto parts store, where normal inventory consists of perhaps 15,000 different stockable items.

Many in small business may feel they do not have the time to explore these costs with precision because of the load of work required to do so. As a result, they strive for some overall turn-over rate which may be right or wrong. If we asssume that the EOQ determined by the formula is the best quantity to make or buy, what happens to our costs if we buy a larger or smaller quantity?

Exhibit 32

*COST OF BEING WRONG ON ORDERING	
% of EOQ Bought	Inventory Cost, Percent of EOQ cost
10%	405%
20%	160%
33%	67%
50%	25%
80%	3%
100%	0% (minimum point)
125%	3%
200%	25%
300%	67%
500%	160%
1,000%	405%

*From Heyel (ed.), *Encyclopedia of Management*, 2nd ed., 1973.

One can see from the table above that going below 80% or above 125% of the Economical Order Quantity can become quite expensive. Since this is the case, one would be well advised to use the EOQ formula for all important items. This, of course, begs the question of what defines an important item. One could say that every item is important, else it would not have been purchased. We can, perhaps, agree with this in a somewhat limited fashion, but qualifying our agreement to the extent that, even while all may be important to some degree, some items may be more important than others.

But, one may ask, how does one gage differences in importance? An unsatisfied customer due to an out-of-stock situation is a dissatisfied customer who may never return. Attempting to stock every sort of item that anyone might possibly need would be prohibitively costly in locked-up capital. Yet, to maintain investment in inventory at reasonable levels, some risk of a stockout situation must be assumed. A policy of forcing some arbitrary annual rate of inventory turnover (or inventory age) will inevitably result in higher costs than necessary. Compromises are essential.

The so-called ABC sytem offers such a compromise. If one lists each type of item sold, in descending order of total annual dollar sales, one very likely finds that about the top 15% of the items will account for about 60% of the total dollars involved in the list, the middle 25% of the items account for perhaps 30% of the dollars, and the bottom 60% of the items will account for only about 10% of the total.

The top 15% of the items are then Class A items, deserving the closest of attention and control. For such items, careful and thorough attention should be given to strict observance of Economical Order Quantities (EOQ). Using EOQ will almost always result in a cost within about 3% of optimum.

Class B items (the middle group) deserve less detailed attention, and perhaps can be handled on an arbitrary rate of inventory turnover. Spot-checking a few Class C items may soon result in the decision that these need little or no attention except to reorder when stock runs out.

The classification of items can and should be modified by the quantity sold, and the frequency with which it is demanded. In many cases, use of the total dollar criterion will take care of this, except where there is a very wide spread in unit price between the highest and lowest items. In a large business, one can and should look at the dollars involved. A small business is much more dependent upon the feelings and satisfaction of the individual customer. Consequently, this restricted view must be modified in consideration of satisfying customer demand to a reasonable extent.

In any case, there is always some penalty connected with a stockout situation. This may be anything from a minor delay to the loss of an order or of a customer. If the probable cost of a stockout can be identified and determined (as it should be), an appropriate risk (or allowable percentage chance) of stockout can be established by the following equation.

Acceptable Chance of Stockout

Where:

EOQ = Economical Order Quantity (as above)
H = Annual Percentage cost of holding inventory
C = Cost per unit, dollars
M = Monthly usage, in dollars
K = Dollar cost of a stockout situation
$\%$ = Percent chance of a stockout

Equation 23:

$$\% = \frac{100 \times EOQ \times H \times C}{12 \times M \times K}$$

Effective use of working capital is always a problem for any business, and the smaller the business, the larger the working capital problem becomes. Making use of an ABC inventory classification system, plus careful attention to EOQ in ordering Class A items and accepting a reasonable risk of a stockout situation on some items will tend to assure greater effectiveness of working capital use. A chart for determining reordering points is included below.

3. ESSENTIALS OF PRODUCTION PLANNING AND CONTROL

The total productive process, in manufacturing, generally involves integrating the "Four M's of Management"; Money, Materials, Men, and Machines to produce a saleable product or service. Our main thrust in this book has been on Money, on the financial aspects. However, making sales promises is of little avail unless there is a saleable product capable of being made at an acceptable cost, sold at an acceptable profit, and delivered reasonably close to on time.

We have previously discussed use of the Operation Sheet as one of the fundamental sources of production planning, together with the

Exhibit 33

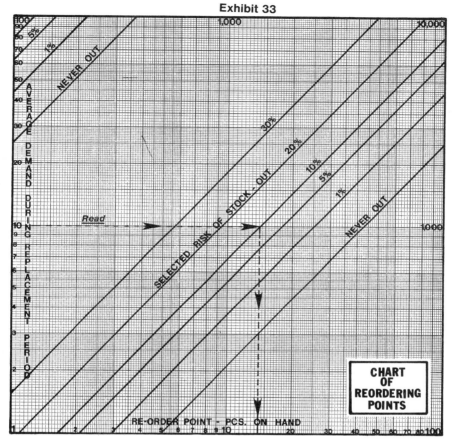

Product Tree, flow charts, flow-process charts, timestudies and other sources of information from which the production plan is formulated. The exact configuration will vary, of course, with the particular company, product, and market.

Production control deals with the other three "M's"; integration of Men, Materials, and Machines to produce a saleable, profitable product in timely fashion. It is accomplished by imposing a form of feedback control on actual operations through use of a semidigital, semi-analog paperwork model of the production processes.

Following is a diagram of the typical production control system.

One can see that here is another case of feedback loop operation for control purposes. Variations from any production plan are normal and can be expected. Machines break down, deliveries are late, people

Exhibit 34

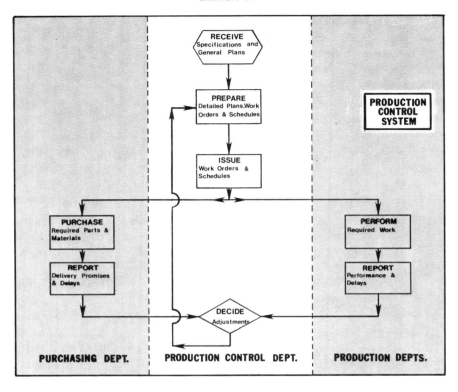

make mistakes, there is spoilage, workers become ill; a thousand and one things can and often do happen to interfere with the smooth progress of a production plan. To attempt to keep the plan on track in spite of these things is the job of production control.

Naturally, in developing feedback controls, the first thing needed is sensory mechanisms to detect deviations from the plan. In the case of production control, these are production reports as to what was or was not completed. In other words, what happened.

Getting this information quickly is a major source of difficulty to many companies, and as we have mentioned many times, any delays or slowness in determining what happened complicate decision making, and often result in wrong decisions.

The customary answer to some of these problems is the maintenance of some "safety stock" in inventory, in excess of current needs, and to cover operations while replacement stock is obtained. In the previous section on inventory control, we made no mention of safety stock, suggesting that some level of stockout possibility must be accepted, for the cost penalties of maintaining an inventory level sufficient to assure "never out" are generally prohibitive.

We maintain the suggestion that some risk of potential stockout must be accepted. However, to establish this level, we need to know what the cost penalty of a particular item being out of stock may be. This was mentioned earlier. What needs to be done is a comparison between the cost of maintaining various levels of extra inventory and the cost of a stockout.

To this point we have not dealt effectively with determining the penalty or cost of a stockout situation. This includes the opportunity cost of the profit from lost sales, the management cost of the facilities and manpower idled because of the stockout, plus any premium costs incurred in eliminating the stockout condition. Any or all of these can become very severe at times.

A very clear manufacturing example was dealt with by a professional colleague some years ago. The problem involved an automated production line for packaging table salt for sale in grocery stores. The line involved winding the box from newsboard, stamping the spout from a coil of sheet metal, stamping end caps from newsboard, assembling one cap to the box body, filling the box with salt, inserting the spout in the other end cap and sealing it, applying the second end cap to the filled box, applying a paper label, and packing the filled boxes into cases made from coiled rolls of corrugated board.

This had been planned as a continuous process, with automated conveyor transport between work stations and from the end of the line to the shipping department. However, the line was able to achieve only about 20% of its planned production.

The problem was soon isolated. Transportation between work stations was direct and immediate. Shut downs were required from time to time at the various work stations to replenish material, clean up glue, eliminate jams, make adjustments, and other similar things. A shut-down of any work station meant a shut-down of the entire line.

The solution was ridiculously simple; after making a study to determine the average shut-down time at each station, conveyor loops were installed between each work station made long enough to hold a sufficient supply to maintain the following operation in production for 90% of the shutdowns which were likely. This, of course increased in-process inventory, and added to holding cost. However, total output of the line promptly increased to approximately 90% of its capacity. The change in unit cost is obvious, and was well worth the safety stock added to the line.

Another problem in the manufacturing business is that of providing enough excess material at the beginning of the process to take care of attrition in the production process due to spoiled work and waste. This represents additional cost, and must be controlled, yet attrition losses must be compensated if deliveries are to be maintained. Again the concept of safety stock is often adopted in the form of an inventory of finished goods to act as a bellows with which to adjust variations in product flow from the factory to a smooth flow to the customer. This represents more investment, and added holding cost which must be considered in planning and pricing for profit.

If the production process is at all complicated, prompt assimilation and handling of a large mass of complex and interrelated data is required. Determination and summarizing the results of a day's happenings in a factory can be a major task, often beyond the physical or financial capacity of many small businesses. Again, development of microcomputers of substantial capacity at reasonable cost offers a partial solution, but lacking stock programs, or programming capability more or less "in-house," progress in using this avenue to handle the data is quite limited as yet.

In summation, Production Control is a classic example of the operation of feedback control. Colloquially speaking, here it is.

- PLANNING
  "Now, here is what we want to do."

- SENSING
  "What happened?"

- EXPLORING ALTERNATIVES
  "Well, what do we do now?"

- DECIDING
  "OK, I guess this looks like the best bet."

- CORRECTING

  "Here's the change order."

- RESENSING

  "Did it work?"

Fine tuning this process to make maximum effective use of capital and to maximize profit requires that this process operate very rapidly, and in light of the probabilities involved. Methods for evaluating alternatives and making decisions are included in Chapter 11.

4. PROBLEMS OF REVIEW, CHANGE, AND ADJUSTMENT

Inability to handle large masses of data and to perform complex calculations quickly has deterred and actually prevented many small business people from taking advantage of the advances in management science. This inability has placed small business at an increasing disadvantage in competition with larger enterprises with the financial and personnel abilities to use these techniques to decrease the need for the substantial margin for error that was previously available to the smaller business.

As this ability to deal successfully with large amounts of detailed information is developed, the financing and decision making of an organization or of an individual becomes more and more finely tuned and more and more capable of discerning and taking advantage of small improvements, while decreasing the area and risk of potential error in decision making.

The problems of control and proper review of a complex operation can be substantial, and at times overpowering. The amount of data and complex calculations involved in using modern management science make it almost impossible for the average small businessman to use it without the benefit of help. However, the recent advances in computer technology with its ability to handle large masses of data quickly have placed this form of aid within the effective financial reach of many small business people.

The main problem as of this writing is one of the availability of suitable computer programs and report formats to fit the needs of many small businesses. Stock programs are slowly being developed, but many are not yet in condition to be widely useful; further, sources for programming to adjust stock programs to the peculiar needs of an individual business are not readily available, and their cost is often unaffordable to small business. This places the burden of making such adjustments on the owner-manager, who then, in addition to everything else, must learn to become a programmer.

A secondry problem is that of developing an awareness of this potential in the small businessman together with sufficient education in management science and its applications for him to ask the right questions.

Many managers in small business today are becoming aware of the need to refine and improve their knowledge and managerial skills, and are seeking added information on use of modern management techniques. Colleges and universities are becoming more and more aware of the need, and are constructing courses and programs to fill the need.

A more serious problem in effecting change, however, is that which may be labeled "Psychological Inertia." This may be equated with habit, to some extent. Many people tend to resist change, for they find it disturbing. It introduces potential incertainties to them which did not previously exist. It forces them to do different things, and to think in a different manner at times.

Sir Isaac Newton defined the property of physical inertia as the tendency of a body at rest to remain at rest, and a body in motion to remain in motion in the same direction, unless acted upon by application of some exterior force. This can be well described as, in effect, resistance to change.

It also aptly describes what happens to people who have become accustomed to act and to think in established patterns. Habit and psychological inertia affect both worker and supervisor. It is easy to operate by habit, but thinking and the exercise of care to operate a new method in opposition to established habit can be indeed difficult, both physically and emotionally. And, since it is difficult, it is resisted.

In fact, it has been said, with or without justification, that inability to accept and deal with change is a major problem in the employment of older workers. It may be inaccurate to ascribe such resistance only to older workers, but ingrained habit is indeed difficult to change.

Such inertia also effects the ability of an executive or manager to develop changes, for it often serves to set limits on the freedom of his imagination to roam fully in search of some innovation or cost reduction. Habits of one sort or another exist in almost everyone, and may well have more effect upon the actions of a person than he or she realizes. It does require a conscious effort of some magnitude to move out of a habit into some new procedure or thought process.

Indeed, there may even be a fear factor in resistance to change. People do tend to fear and suspect the unknown and the new, and in attempting to effect change, the manager must deal with this problem.

Along with these tendencies is that of the ability of people in general to accept and deal with only a limited amount of change at any one time. To be effective, major changes must often be instituted (or administered) in measured doses, so as not to exceed the tolerance of the people affected.

A feeling of instability and constant change can cause serious morale problems, or a feeling of interest and excitement, depending upon how it is presented, and how it is perceived by those affected. As we mentioned earlier at several points, what a person perceives is true to him, regardless of fact.

With these psychological problems, instituting and effecting change becomes a subject demanding considerable care and thought on the part of any business owner, executive, or manager. A careful appraisal of the amount and direction of change must be made, with reference to the emotional impact on those involved, and with reference to the amount of change which can be tolerated at any one time by those affected.

At times, this can become a major problem, for the capacity and willingness of people to accept change frequently does not coincide with the real demands of the situation from a financial and business welfare point of view. Care in presentation, and frequent compromises may be required.

10. Management Controls

1. FLEXIBLE BUDGETING

It has been well said that to control the purse is to control the person. In an equivalent sense, a major mission of management is the control and effective use of the money of the business. Using it wisely and minimizing waste is a task of extreme importance.

In the task of controlling the use of money, budgeting is an important tool. Yet, setting up budgets can be an agonizing, time-consuming task, which oftentimes is resented by the lower echelons of management. A frequent source of resentment, also, in the case of traditional budget setting, is that the budget does not take into account changing demands caused by more or less normal fluctuations in productive activities and sales.

In our preceding discussion of the methods of analyzing cost behavior, we have also developed an effective basis from which we can design a way to deal with these problems; a flexible budget, rather than the traditional type. In looking at cost behavior, we found both fixed and variable components. The mathematics of regression gives us these in quantitative form, as constants in mathematical formulas which we can then apply to the budgeting problem.

Budgets may be established for use at several different levels within an organization. Of primary importance, of course, is the overall budget for the entire organization. This is one of the main instruments by which the plans of management may be implemented. Naturally, it should be established first, and subsidiary budgets for various cost centers or divisions of the operation should flow from it.

The company's philosophy of budgeting is an important consideration. If improperly used, budgets can harm as well as aid operation of the business. At times, budgets are interpreted as absolute limits, rather than as guides, and when this happens, needed flexibility in day-to-day operations can be seriously impaired.

A budget should act as a planned course, similar in concept to that used by a seaman, or an airplane pilot to navigate toward a desired destination. In making the journey, winds shift, and sometimes blow adversely, and adjustments must be made to the direction of travel if the destination is to be reached. So it is with budgets. However, budget adjustments made as a matter of convenience or accommodation without careful thought or planning can destroy control and lose the entire value of the budgeting process.

The flexible budget consists of a formula using a fixed component (when required to permit the enterprise, division, or department to exist) plus a variable component which rises and falls with variations in the activity level of the operational segment being budgeted. This formula is a summation of the fixed and variable components of the various expense accounts as they apply to that operational segment. It may be expressed as a simple figure for the entire profit center or segment under consideration, but is more useful if given in detail with reference to the individual classifications of expense.

The virtue of the flexible budget is that the formula automatically and painlessly adjusts the allowance for expense in each category with variations in the level of productive activity of the sector to which it applies.

In establishing subsidiary budgets for segments or cost centers within the organization, the monetary value of sales is not always the most appropriate measure of the productive activity of the particular segment under consideration.

For example, the value of sales made would have little relationship to the productive activities of a mechanic responsible for maintaining the production line conveyors in good condition. His activities are too far separated both in function and in time for sales to be a useful measure of his worth. Yet, his efforts have a definite bearing on the company's ability to produce, and, in consequence, a budget for his activities should be established.

In such cases, other types of measurement may be needed, such as a monetary allowance for maintenance of conveyors based on the number of plant operating hours, or some such measure more directly reflective of the degree and type of productive activity for which a budget is being provided. Means of establishing such measures will be discussed in later sections dealing with Employee Motivation and Incentives.

The important factor is that the budget for a particular department or profit center be directly related to the productive activity level of that particular operational segment, and that it state allowances for factors which are within the span of control of that segment.

Capital expenditures for tooling, equipment, methods improvement, and similar projects also need to be budgeted for evaluation, planning, and control purposes. The same methods of evaluation should be used to establish probable costs and timing of savings or other gains as were recommended for evaluating job improvements. The difference is that these projections will often reach futher into the future and will need to be coupled with forecasts of future business and its income-producing capacity.

2. VARIANCE REPORTING

Earlier, we discussed use of the feedback loop as a means of control. You will remember that the first thing to be done in operating a feedback loop is to sense deviations from plan. We are now going to consider another direct business application of these principles.

A budget, or set of flexible budget formulas, constitutes a plan for effective use of the monetary resources of the business in carrying out its planned operations. To institute control, a means of sensing deviations from plan is necessary. This is the function of the Variance Report.

Typically, a variance report shows, for each type of expense, the actual amount of expense incurred, the budgeted amount for that expense, and any difference, over, or under budget. Such a report is shown as Exhibit 35 below.

Such a report, if produced in a timely fashion, supplies the sensing of deviations from the plan (budget), from which management can make the necessary decisions as to the direction and extent of correction to be applied.

Exhibit 35

<table>
<tr><td colspan="4" align="center">OPERATING STATEMENT

XYZ COMPANY

MONTH ENDING
June 30,1979</td></tr>
<tr><td>ACCOUNT</td><td>ACTUAL</td><td>BUDGET</td><td>VARIANCE</td></tr>
<tr><td>Net Sales</td><td>3,992,758</td><td>-----------</td><td>---------</td></tr>
<tr><td>Cost of Goods Sold</td><td>2,680,298</td><td>2,595,293</td><td>(85,005)</td></tr>
<tr><td>Gross Profit</td><td>1,312,460</td><td>1,397,465</td><td>(85,005)</td></tr>
<tr><td>Selling Expense</td><td>227,600</td><td>205,300</td><td>(22,300)</td></tr>
<tr><td>Administrative Expense</td><td>496,745</td><td>493,678</td><td>(3,067)</td></tr>
<tr><td>Misc. Expense</td><td>77,050</td><td>78,923</td><td>1,873</td></tr>
<tr><td>Depreciation</td><td>111,509</td><td>111,509</td><td>--------</td></tr>
<tr><td>Interest Expense</td><td>85,274</td><td>87,128</td><td>1,854</td></tr>
<tr><td>Total Expense</td><td>998,178</td><td>976,538</td><td>21,640</td></tr>
<tr><td>Income Before Taxes</td><td>314,282</td><td>420,927</td><td>(106,145)</td></tr>
<tr><td>Taxes</td><td>163,708</td><td>218,882</td><td>55,174</td></tr>
<tr><td>Income After Taxes</td><td>150,574</td><td>202,045</td><td>(51,471)</td></tr>
<tr><td>Dividends to Owners</td><td>92,300</td><td>92,300</td><td>--------</td></tr>
<tr><td>Add to Retained Earn.</td><td>58,274</td><td>109,745</td><td>(51,471)</td></tr>
<tr><td colspan="4">Unfavorable variances are shown: (0,000,000)</td></tr>
</table>

The report shown in Exhibit 35 is very much in summary form, and lacks the detail of individual expense account variance which should appear on an income statement for use by operating personnel. As a consequence, major variances are easier to see than might otherwise be the case, but the detail for lower echelons is missing.

Other types of variance reports, such as reports of job progress as compared with schedule, reports of project expenditures as compared with schedule, or even of rejected work are necessary to control and operate a business successfully, in addition to budget variance reports as such. These are the sensing mechanisms by which control can be exercised.

3. TOLERANCED VARIANCES AND MANAGEMENT BY EXCEPTION

Historically, accounting reports have shown every variance, no matter how large or small. Naturally, all variances should theoretically be matters for management attention; favorable ones for praise of subordinates, unfavorable ones for constructive criticism. However, in a practical sense, many variances are so minor as to be safely ignored, while others may be acute, and even call for emergency action.

There is a mode of management operation which has been advanced by many in recent years as a means of clarifying the areas to which management should apply its attentions. This is called **Management by Exception.**

Management is always required to spread its attentions over many different aspects of operation, and in so doing, particularly in smaller businesses, often has difficulty in distinguishing the important from the trivial. All too often, managers find themselves drowning in trivialities, "putting out fires" all day long, at the expense of giving proper attention to matters of real and lasting importance. This is particularly true of the manager or owner of a small business who does not have the resources to hire enough specialists. The principle of management by exception, if operated properly, tends to relieve this situation.

The fundamental assumption under which this principle operates is that one should not be concerned with trivialities, nor give more than very limited attention to those aspects of the business which are running well. Instead, assuming that all is well and proceeding according to plan unless notified otherwise, management can devote direct attention only to situations where substantial deviations from plan occur.

Of course, to make management by exception effective, management must have a system of reports which will allow it to sense substantial deviations from plan with sufficient promptness to permit effective correction. Note that this again uses the feedback principle of sensing and control.

To operate under the management by exception principle, making use of variance reports as a sensing mechanism can be somewhat difficult under conventional modes of reporting, since the trivial is shown as well as the substantial. Management then must face the difficulty of distinguishing the important from the trivial differences in scanning the report. To make management by exception meaningful, there must be some definition of normality and of exceptions.

To supply such a definition, a concept from the world of modern manufacturing is offered. This is the concept of the use of tolerances. As applied in manufacturing, this concept implies that there exists some amount by which dimensions may be permitted to vary from the established norm yet still be acceptable and permit safe and effective operation without harm to the intended function.

In applying the concept of tolerancing to variance reports and to the principle of management by exception, it is proposed that the variances which are within established tolerances be suppressed from the variance report, leaving only the out-of-tolerance variances for consideration by management.

Let us look again at Exhibit 35. Although it is a very much condensed version of an operating statement, we can see that there are some significant variances, which should immediately catch the eye of management.

First there is the unfavorable variance of $85,005 in the Cost of Goods Sold. Several possibilities suggest themselves as causes for this variance. There is the possibility of labor inefficiency. Second, there is the possibility of unanticipated cost changes in materials or related expense. There can have been inventory write-offs, and there could have been engineering changes not reflected in pricing, to mention a few. Certainly, such a variance would seem to warrant detailed investigation.

However, here is where the principle of tolerancing might enter. This variance only amounted to 3.28% of budget. Should management concern itself with an item only varying from plan by 3%? Possibly so, in this particular case, since the cost of goods sold is a major expense, and a 1% variance involves much more money than the total budget for some minor expense accounts.

Another major variance is in the cost of Selling. Again, this particular cost is one which often constitutes a major portion of expense, and special attention could well be deserved. In this case, the variance amounted to 10.86% of budget; certainly a significant variance demanding immediate attention.

The variances in Administrative Expense, and in Miscellaneous Expense are relatively nominal, and probably should have been suppressed in the interest of focusing attention on more important items.

The final variance in income after taxes and in retained earnings is vastly important, and can arouse stockholder indignation, even though dividends had been paid, because of the loss of stockholder equity from the planned level.

In analyzing account behavior, as with the behavior of profits, there is usually some random variation from month to month, which creates a band of uncertainty around the trend lines developed. It could be useful in establishing tolerances for variances from budget if management were to consider the extent of these random variations from pattern, and establish tolerance limits based on accepting some agreed percentage of risk that a variance will be outside the established limits. A convenient tolerance by this method would be that of plus or minus one standard deviation, giving a 68% probability of any variance being within tolerance, and a 32% probability of being out of tolerance and being flagged for management attention.

Consideration should be given, however, not only to the degree of chance, but also to the magnitude of the amount of money involved in the probable variances as well. If the monetary value is significant, a tighter tolerance range should be imposed.

What makes the principle of tolerancing practical in manufacturing is that variations from exactness of dimension in the manufacturing of parts, so long as they are within the required tolerance, will occur in random fashion when assembled so that the final assembly or "stack" of parts will be usable and function properly.

However, there is always the possibility that all the parts in a particular assembly could happen to be either on the large side or the small side of their tolerances, with the result that the finished stack would be unserviceable due to the one-sided accumulation of tolerances. This problem is taken care of by establishing a dimensional tolerance for the finished assembly.

Application of the principle of tolerancing to the budget variances can result in similar behavior; i.e., a series of one sided, in-tolerance variances can accumulate to an out-of-tolerance result. Consequently, an overall tolerance for variance from budget should be established to highlight any one-sided accumulation of in-tolerance variances.

In summary, most of the techniques suggested to this point have been oriented toward exposing areas of potential or real difficulty more clearly, so that the attentions of management can be focused directly upon them rather than being diffused over minor matters of little effect upon the continuing profitable operation of the business.

4. ZERO BASE BUDGETING

Among the recent advances in management technique is the concept of zero base budgeting. This is an example of the use of some catch words to put a new face on a long-standing principle; applied good common sense. The idea behind zero base budgeting is extremely sound, and stems from the need to deal with a common human problem of habit or, as we have labeled it so that we may sound scholarly (!), "psychological inertia."

As mentioned previously, Newton's law of physical inertia states that a body at rest will remain at rest unless disturbed by application of some force, and that a body in motion will remain in motion in the same direction unless disturbed by the application of some force. This can be paraphrased into Hogsett's law:

THE EXISTING STATE OF AFFAIRS TENDS TO CONTINUE OR GET WORSE UNLESS SOMEONE DOES SOMETHING ABOUT IT.

We see this inertia present in a psychological fashion in many aspects of our life. A decision made by a judge sets a precedent, and forever after, lawyers are quoting that precedent as justification for their cases. A number or sentence committed to paper becomes sacred and is quoted as authority. Memos and reports, which might have been needed for some special reason continue to be prepared as routine long after the need for them has passed.

Indeed, we are talking about habit, which removes the need for decision making, and leads to the acceptance of things as they are simply because they are. To a business, this often means the gradual accumulation of excessive cost, lack of adjustment to environmental changes, and, in some cases, even fatality.

The best remedy for psychological inertia is the maintenance by management of a consistent attitude of **CONSTRUCTIVE DISSAT-ISFACTION,** as has been previously recommended.

Zero base budgeting is an example of the very type of tactic needed to reinforce this more useful attitude of constructive dissatisfaction. Management simply says, "We will not allocate any money to this area of expense unless it is proved to be essential. Under no circumstances will we approve an expenditure merely because we have done so in the past."

Even though management may know that some expenditures will be required for an essential need, demanding complete justification will often cause sufficient inspection and thought about ways of satisfying the need to trim the amount requested. This demand for new justification tends to diminish the creeping cost increases which often become so troublesome.

The idea of using constructive dissatisfaction to counteract psychological inertia permeates the entire range of the thought processes of industrial engineering and management science.

The refusal to accept things as they are and have been is responsible for many of our economic and social advances.

The positive aspects of **CONSTRUCTIVE DISSATISFACTION** need emphasis. Many people are critical and dissatisfied, and cry for "a better way" about one or another aspect of life and times, but do nothing constructive about their complaints, except to complain more loudly. This nagging type of behavior usually accomplishes nothing, except perhaps to increase the level of general irritation.

Conversely, the constructively dissatisfied person says, "This is wrong. There has to be a better way, and I'm going to find it." And then he goes to work on his search.

Strangely enough, with adequate expenditure of mental and physical perspiration (and occasional use of judiciously selected four-letter words !) real improvements are made.

Not only does this type of person succeed for himself, but often pulls the remainder of the organization with him by example, to the great benefit of all concerned.

11. Evaluating Changes

1. THE COSTS OF CHANGE

As was mentioned earlier, change for the sake of change generally proves costly. Change should be contemplated only when the facts are clear, and there is a useful advantage to be gained. We shall now discuss various ways by which the advantages and disadvantages of various changes may be evaluated.

Any change involves cost, even if only that of the time required to evaluate it. Often, in contemplating the making of some change or proposed improvement, its designer falls in love with his proposal, and fails to investigate all the potential costs which may be involved in putting the proposal into effect. This form of wishful thinking can be a trap for the unwary management.

One frequently overlooked cost which should be considered in evaluating any proposal for change is that of the potential benefits which would have been derived from alternatives which were foregone and foreclosed by the selected change. Another is the potential cost of the disruptions to previously established lines of action caused by the change. This can include the cost of retraining employees, a slow-down of production, a slow-down of deliveries, a decline in income, employee dissatisfaction resulting in low morale, and even in strikes, and a host of other possibilities.

It is extremely important that management be fully aware of all of the costs involved in implementing a proposal for change. It must be kept in mind that while many changes may hold the potential for future benefit, the cost of making changes occurs in the immediate present, as well as the future. Change always requires some kind of immediate investment.

For example, if the pay for an industrial engineer is $10.00 per hour, and fringe costs are another $2.50 per hour, the "direct labor" cost of making improvements would be $12.50 per hour. If the company needs to make a 20% return on funds employed, the minimum target for the industrial engineer would be to accomplish about $15.65 of cost reduction for each hour of work, over and above any cost for tools, materials, or other expense required to accomplish the required improvement.

This may seem a severe task and certainly overstates the appropriate level of responsibility for the industrial engineer. Some tempering is in order, for industrial engineers are often also responsible for establishing and maintaining various types of feedback control systems, which have great value in permitting sound control of operations. These added benefits should be credited against the cost of having the industrial engineering resource.

Nonetheless, on a broader scale, the hard standard of profitability should always be in view. Anything which is done must truly earn its way if the business is to remain sound.

It is often good, when considering a change, for some member of management with a good imagination and understanding of the problem to take a deliberately antagonistic position toward the proposed change, for the purpose of assuring that all the real and potential costs are entered into consideration. There are times when even a "Devil's Advocate" is useful.

The effects upon project costs of the span of time over which the cost should be recovered has not been considered. This aspect will be discussed in the next section.

2. EVALUATING BENEFITS AND INVESTMENTS

Improvements are normally judged by how much they will cost versus how much they will earn over some period of time. The "Payout Time" is the most common statement made: "This will pay for itself in —— days, months, or years." Interpreted, this means that the total cost or investment is divided by the estimated saving per day, month, or year to obtain the payout period.

This introduces a possibility of some degree of deception, since it does not take into account the time value of money. Making studies of improvements, or making the improvements themselves demands the immediate spending of money or the accruing of cost. Yet those costs can only be recovered at a later date, or through savings accomplished over some future period of time. As we have seen previously, money in hand is worth more than money to be received in the future.

Therefore, to be realistic, proposed savings should be discounted to their present value before being compared with the immediate cost of the investment to obtain them. However, we have a different situation from the one we saw in holding inventory and accounts receivable.

Instead of a lump sum to be returned at some future time, we are now required to deal with a series of incomes or an income stream to be received over the proposed period of time to recover the cost. Naturally, the near term cash flows, incomes, or savings are worth more to us than those progressively further out into the future.

There are two methods for achieving this discounting of the income stream so as to supply a reasonable basis for choosing among alternatives, or making a go, no-go decision. These are:

1. Net Present Value
2. Internal Rate of Return

The cash flow from methods improvement is actually continuous during periods of operation, but can be considered to come in periodic payments, one each accounting period. As each successive payment occurs at a progressively greater amount of time from the time of investment, each must be discounted individually according to the elapsed time, and the results totaled over the entire time span. The payout period for the investment in a methods improvement would therefore be that time necessary for the discounted savings to equal the initial investment. The following formula applies.

Present Value of Cash Flow Series

Where: PV = Present value of total income
r = Required or Target rate of return

t = Payment Number
CF_t = Amount of Payment t
I = Original investment or cost
n = Number of Cash Flows (the highest value of t)

Equation 24:

$$PV = \underset{t=1}{\overset{n}{SUM}} \left\{ \frac{CF_{tn}}{(1 + r)} \right\}$$

In the case of the Internal Rate of Return, this rate is that which, when applied, will yield a present value equal to the required investment or cost. The relationship is expressed by the same equation, but solved for r. The resulting rate may then be compared with the rate of return on funds employed needed to meet the company's profit target.

Solving this equation manually can become quite time-consuming, even with the use of the Table of Values of $1 per Year at Rate r, (Appendix) since each payment must be discounted individually at several different rates in order to zero in on an approximately correct rate.

Computer programs for solving the Internal Rate of Return problem are built into some hand-held calculators, such as the Texas Instruments TI-59 models.

If a choice between several alternatives is required, a desirability index can be computed by means of the following equation.

Desirability Index

Where:

DI = Desirability Index
PV = Present Value of Income Stream
I = Initial Investment or Cost

Equation 25: $DI = \dfrac{PV}{I}$

This results in being able to apply the following rule for making go, no-go decisions, or selecting among many alternatives.

DECISION RULES

1. If DI > 1.00, GO; else NO Go.

2. If alternatives exist, select highest DI

With this type of quantitative decision rule, the user is assured of selecting the optimal alternative, provided that he has entered factual data into the equations rather than data resulting from wishful thinking.

3. EVALUATING DECISIONS

Earlier, in Chapter 2, we discussed the desirability of using facts, instead of guesses, and using them in an organized, systematic fashion in the making of decisions. As was discussed, at any point when a decision is required, there are at least two alternatives: yes, and no; go, or no-go. Usually there are also other possibilities, both in kinds of action or inaction to be taken, and in the possible range of operation of the various exterior, or uncontrollable factors which act on the problem.

In making any decision, we are making an immediate projection into the future. The decisions made now cannot affect the past; it is irretrievable. They cannot affect the present, for it is but an instant, passing during the very act of making the decision. Of the future, we have no certainty. We can only make assumptions, and appraise probabilities.

By use of forecasts, reason, analysis, and measurement, we must seek to predict the future with a sufficient degree of accuracy that we will be right more often than we will be wrong, and that we will profit thereby, rather than lose. Therefore, we have been led to look for patterns in past behavior.

The existence of a pattern of past behavior tends to simplify our forecasting problem somewhat, in that we can have some expectation that the pattern will repeat. While this is not necessarily true in the real world, when patterns occur, they tend to diminish the absolute randomness of uncertainty as to the future. As we have seen in forecasting, the amount of variability around a trend can be expressed also in terms of the probability of future incidents being within certain ranges of the trend indication.

The effect of all of this is that most of the time, we, as managers, are making our decisions and plans to a greater or lesser degree under conditions of uncertainty.

We have no way of being absolutely certain that something will or will not happen in the future. Under these conditions, it is entirely natural to seek ways of gaining greater accuracy and soundness in our decisions, so as to minimize the damage resulting from being wrong, and increasing the profit from being right.

The decision problem has a structure composed of the following elements.

1. DECISION MAKER. There is someone, either a person, association, group, or organization, vested with the responsibility (and hopefully, the authority) for making the decision.

2. ALTERNATIVES. At least two alternatives exist, between which a choice must be made. With only one alternative, there is no choice and no decision. Very often in the small business area, it is a real problem to determine if there are alternatives.

3. EVENTS. Occurrences which will affect achievement of the objectives, or affect the results of the decision in a way beyond the control of the decision maker. They include a series of independent, mutually exclusive, and complete set of possible outcomes, only one of which can occur.

4. PAYOFF. The result of an event pursuant to a decision which is of positive or negative benefit to the decision maker. A way of evaluating decision alternatives is by comparison of payoffs from those various alternatives.

5. UNCERTAINTY. The indefiniteness concerning which of the possible events or outcomes will occur. The degree of certainty is

expressed by a decimal number (less than 1) indicating the known or estimated probability of its occurrence on a percentage basis. We can call this the odds, or the number of chances out of 100 that something will or will not happen.

We are indebted to Morris Hamburg of the Wharton School of the University of Pennsylvania who laid out this array of explanation in his text *Statistical Analysis for Decision Making*.

The next problem is to determine what criteria will be used to evaluate payoff results. There are several different criteria which could be adopted as a basis for judging the correct strategy among the various alternatives, and in light of the various possible alternative events.

The **"Least Damage"** criterion, or the **"Maximin,"** operates on the basis of pessimism. It assumes that Nature and chance will be unfavorable, so the decision-maker looks at the various payoffs to determine which alternative will yield the least harm if things were to go badly.

The **"Maximum Expected Profit"** criterion, like the others, depends upon making use of the expected probability of the various events. This is achieved by computing the expected or weighted value of the potential results from each of the alternative events or conditions which may operate.

Another potential criterion is the **Expected Opportunity Loss,** which can be described as the loss resulting from failure to adopt the best possible action. This is expressed as the difference in payoffs between that of the act selected versus the best possible act for a given event or circumstance.

A fourth criterion is **Minimax Opportunity Loss** which again considers Nature and chance to be inimical, so selection is made on the basis of minimizing damage from the worst possible opportunity loss.

These criteria may seem a bit confusing at this point, and clarification will probably best be done by means of a decision example. Before doing so, however, another point needs to be made.

We are compelled to inquire how we obtain the respective probabilities of the occurrence of the various events under consideration. The first source is exploration of past behavior of the various possible events and of the frequency of their occurrence. If there is a pattern of behavior in evidence, there is some chance that it will repeat. If there is a certain already demonstrated range of probability, it should be used.

Failing this, however, the decision-maker is faced with making an educated guess. This is not all bad, even though it seems to fly in the face of our pressure for measured fact.

Actually, a person in business soon develops certain "gut feelings" about the factors affecting his business, and often can do a good job of estimating the relative probability of various events. At worst, we can begin by assuming equal probability for all the potential events, then testing the results.

A good way of testing, when the odds are in doubt, is to change the odds slightly and see what changes happen in the result. A few trials of this type will give good guidance as to the likely effect of errors in estimating the probabilities, and thus aid in clarifying the actual decision. In scholarly circles, this is known as "sensitivity analysis," testing the sensitivity of the answer to changes in the conditions of the problem, and it is applied to many different types of analytical and probability based procedures.

To clarify the matter of selection of criteria, let us walk through an example.

Let us assume that we have a manufacturing plant, and are dissatisfied with the level of profits. We have decided that we can afford to spend $5000 to attempt to achieve improvement. We have a choice of spending that money on an advertising campaign to increase sales, or on overtime payments to our industrial engineers to conduct a special campaign of cost reduction.

In looking at our sample company, we find that its previous history indicates that a cost reduction campaign can with certainty be expected to show a minimum improvement of 10% in profit as a percentage of sales within a period of one year. Present profits are averaging 10% of sales. The Sales Manager predicts that the advertising campaign has a 75% chance of improving the present sales level (which amounts to $785,000 per year) by about 12%. We find that the cost of money is averaging 12% per year, or 1% per month.

First, let us attempt to evaluate the cost reduction program. A 10% improvement in a 10% rate of profit on sales is equivalent to 1% of sales (10% of $785,000 = $78,500; 10% improvement = 10% of $78,500) which equals a gross of $7850 less a cost of $5000, yielding a net of $2850 as the expected gain from spending the money on cost reduction. This net profit is not immediately available, and will not be fully realized for a year. We have instead an income stream of $237.50 per month. We must discount this to account for the time value of money. Applying the formula given in the previous section covering discounting cash flows, we find a net present value of $2684.33 for this saving.

Now let us examine the real value of the advertising. If the campaign succeeds as predicted, we would realize an increase in sales of $94,200, and at our present profit rate (equivalent to 1% of sales), we would expect to realize a profit increase of $9420. One would think that the obvious choice is to start the advertising at once.

Not necessarily! For there is a chance that the campaign will fail. Remember that the Sales Manager gave an estimate of a 75% chance of success (which also means a 25% chance of failure, since the probability of success plus the probability of failure must equal 100% for all chances are covered thereby).

To be realistic, we must therefore **DEVALUE THE EXPECTED PROFIT TO A LEVEL EQUAL TO ITS PROBABILITY OF HAPPENING.** In this case, the $9420 must be devalued to the .75 level, or $7065. Again, deducting our $5000 cost leaves us an expected net profit of $2065. In addition, this sales expansion will not take place at once, but over the next year, so, again, the net must be devalued to present value terms, as previously explained.

One can see that even without determining the present value of the potential sales savings, cost reduction is the better path to pursue. We can question how much the net difference amounts to in present value. Cost reduction yields us an expected net present value of $2684.33, while the Sales plan yields a net present value of only $1936.81.

The difference between the expected values of the two choices amounts to $747.52 in favor of the cost reduction program. Looking at the relative return on investment, cost reduction yields an expected net profit of $2684.33 on an investment of $5000, for a 53.69% return on investment, while the advertising path yields a net expected profit of only $1936.81 for a rate of return of only 38.74%.

Under the usual conditions of uncertainty in which we in business must operate, the probabilities involved must be given consideration. Failure to give such consideration, plus lack of knowledge on the part of customers of the true odds for or against something happening has led to many casino owners in Las Vegas becoming very, very wealthy.

Another type of case might be even more illustrative. A merchant with annual sales of $1 million and an inventory turn-over of four times per year is considering expanding his inventory to double its previous size. To do this he will have to borrow money, which will cost him 15% per year.

At the same time, the country is undergoing inflation, which increases the value of inventory purchased at lower prices. The merchant anticipates that inflation during the next year will probably be about 10%, that it may go as high as 13%, and likely will not be less than 7%, and plans to increase his prices to keep step with inflation. He anticipates that if he delays buying for another year, his cost of goods will increase at least as fast as the inflation rate. His mark-up is 50% of sales, and his net profit has averaged 10% of sales.

Should he take the plunge? Let us see.

With cost of goods at 50% of sales, his cost of goods would be $500,-000, and with four times per year turnover, his average previous inventory value would have been $125,000. To double this, he would have to borrow $125,000, and, at an interest rate of 15% would incur interest costs for one year amounting to $18,750. With a net profit of 10% of sales ($100,000), his profit rate was $.80 per inventory dollar.

If he turned over his enlarged inventory at the same rate as previously, and sold it all, his sales would be $2,200,000, his cost of goods would have been $1,018,750, and his gross profit would then have been $1,181,250. His average inventory would then be $254,686, including interest cost. His net profit would be $220,000, which yields him a ratio of $.863 per dollar of inventory.

It would seem that he should consult his friendly banker at once. However, this conclusion rests on his selling all his inventory. How valid is this conclusion? We do not know. However, we can get a clue by calculating the percentage by which he would have improved his profitability. In this case, it was from $.80 to $.863, a difference of $.063, amounting to 7.875%. We might say, then, that if he saw at least an 82.125% chance of selling all the added inventory at a 10% increase in unit price, he should borrow. Or we could say that he would be safe if he sold more than 82.125% of his inventory at the 10% increase in price. To the extent that he fell short of such a sales level, he would lose.

However, what happens if he does not borrow? His sales would become 1,100,000, his average inventory would become $137,500 due to inflation (which operates at the same rate in either case), his profit would become $110,000, and the ratio of profitability would be maintained at $.80 per dollar of sales; no improvement, but no loss, either.

It is not our purpose here to introduce all the complex ramifications of decision theory. It is our purpose, however, to demonstrate what can be done with a little thought and attention to detail to reduce the fog of uncertainty which surrounds most business decisions.

Previously we have taken a rather hard stand about the interjection of opinions into quantitative analysis of problems. We must repeat this, for wishful thinking and reasoning toward preconceived conclusions has been the downfall of many would-be businessmen. Yet, when hard statistics and probabilities cannot be obtained, the interjection of subjective estimates of probabilities can become very useful, so long as a rigorous attempt is made to state **"what probably will be," NOT "what I wish it to be."**

12. Organization, Motivation, and Incentives

1. ORGANIZATION

It is generally good practice to establish a clear organization structure for any enterprise, as soon as there is more than the proprietor himself involved. Again, this cannot be a static thing, but must be revised at intervals to accommodate changing circumstances and growth.

To maintain the health of any enterprise, clarity and understanding of its organizational structure is of vital importance. The flow of authority, and the designation of areas of responsibility should be clearly delineated.

If any employee is to function successfully, he must understand clearly what his place, duties, responsibilities, and authority are, and the same understanding must exist vis-à-vis these aspects among his fellow employees. Lack of a clear understanding of their respective duties, responsibilities, inter-relationships, authority, and organizational position by employees is one of the major plagues which afflict management. If these are not clear, confusion usually follows, and the harm caused can be of infinite variety.

As organizations developed in size and complexity, effective structuring became of increasing importance. The earliest and most primitive form of organization is the line type of direct command, in which the commander was completely responsible for all aspects of operation of all his subordinates.

It soon became evident that no king or general could be an effective expert in all things. As size increased, so did the amount of detailed planning and support activity. Organizations soon grew beyond the ability of any one person to administer, control, or in some cases, even understand.

Exhibit 36

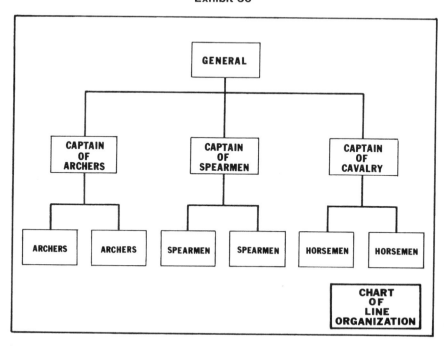

Consequently, a group of advisors and administrative aids and specialists developed. In early stages, this group had no responsibility whatsoever for results, except to the king, and most particularly, had no power of command over the people or the army.

In the early days of management science, a concept of functional management was introduced. In its simplest form, a worker or a soldier had several commanders, each for a specific area of concern. There was a quality boss, a quantity boss, a tool boss, and so on. This never worked out effectively for a very basic reason.

In establishing an organizational structure, it is particularly important to establish command versus advisory responsibility clearly. The structure of command should be particularly clear. Each person should know precisely who his commander is, and should not be subjected to the possibly conflicting commands of two or more different individu-

Exhibit 37

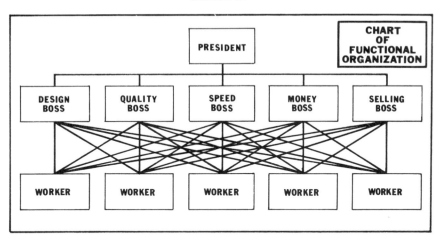

als, as in the case with the functional type of organization, seen above as Exhibit 37.

The advice and commands given by specialists are likely to be biased by their individual concerns. For example, the sales manager will push to make sales, often at the expense of profit. The production manager will want to produce with greatest efficiency, possibly at the expense of sales and/or customer relations or storage costs for inventory. The finance manager will want to minimize risk, minimize credit sales, and concentrate on financial and cash strength. These objectives may well be mutually exclusive unless compromised, and where command of the worker is involved, compromise is not possible until after the conflict has occurred.

Of the various types of organization structure developed over the years, the line and staff type is the most customary. However, the project type is coming more and more into use in certain types of enterprises, particularly in the research and development area.

In most enterprises today, the line and staff concept of organization forms the more or less permanent basis or structure, with the project or task force concept occupying a subordinate and specialized ad hoc position of a somewhat temporary and decidedly flexible nature. Often the task forces or project teams are broken up and reformed to suit the varying needs of different projects or tasks. Even under this concept,

Exhibit 38

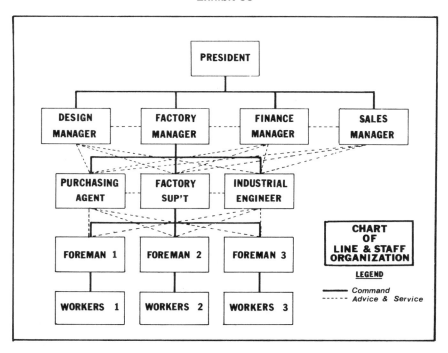

however, within the team, it remains of prime importance to assure proper understanding of the responsibilities and authority of the task force members. It is the top commander's or company president's responsibility to adjust and reconcile these sometimes conflicting views into operating plans and objectives in the most direct pursuit of the goals of the enterprise.

The best practice is to construct a written organization chart, such as those shown above as Exhibit 38, which spells out clearly the flow of authority and responsibility, as well as the inter-relationship of subordinate positions. In establishing an organization structure, consideration should be given to assuring that authority and responsibility are coequal in operation, and that to the maximum extent, responsibilities are so arranged as to take advantage of the personal strengths and to minimize the effect of personal weaknesses of each employee.

As the organization grows and the relationship between top management and the lowest ranked employee becomes more and more distant,

Exhibit 39

SAMPLE POSITION DESCRIPTION

TITLE: Store Manager

Under general direction of the General Manager manage the operations of a retail store selling home computers, computer software, supplies, literature, parts, and associated items.

Open and close store at prescribed hours and days. Conduct routine operations, wait on customers, collect for sales, giving credit within guidelines received from General Manager. Record sales, balance and check cash drawer as required. Make bank deposits. Assume profit responsibility for operation of store, making necessary decisions in connnection therewith, but subject to policies established by the General Manager. Receive, store, and disburse stock, maintaining inventory levels within guidelines as directed by general policy. Order items needing replacement. Pay operating bills, balance checkbook.

Supervise and train store personnel. Maintain discipline. Adjust employee status and pay necessary as necessary to maintain effective and profitable operation. Employ and terminate employees as necessary.

Make personal demonstrations of products for customers, both in store and at customer's location. Train customers in computer use and programming. Answer customer complaints and operating and programming problems. Repair and service customer-owned hardware and software as needed within scope of own knowledge and experience, referring major problems to Manufacturer. Arrange stock and displays. Make outside sales, going to customers locations and trade shows to conduct demonstrations and train customers. Set up, conduct, and tear down trade and other demonstrations as necessary. Develop programming and machine operating competence, and well as repair and adjustment knowledge so as to assist customers with all normal problems. Maintain up-to-date knowledge of machines, equipment, and software sold.

Assume full profit responsibility for all aspects of operation of this type of store.

Perform other minor related duties as necessary

Requires special knowledge of computers, computer operation and programming, with the capacity to absorb and make effective use of additional training.

Make necessary decisions related to store operation, subject only to policies laid down by General Manager.

Requires close mental and visual concentration from time to time, with the ability to think in small sequential steps through fairly complex routines. Intense concentration sometimes required, but frequency is limited.

Responsibility is high for cash, inventory, customer contact and maintenance of service and of customer goodwill, as well as full responsibility for profitable operation of the store.

Surroundings are usual office, but is occasionally required to drive to customers premises.

Except for driving and for occasional exposure to electrical shock when repairing machines, hazards are nominal.

formulation of written job descriptions becomes more and more a necessity, in order to minimize confusion. A sample of such a Position Description is shown above as Exhibit 39.

No job description ever written completely described all the duties, obligations, authority, conditions, and other aspects of even the most routine job. And, probably no description ever will. Nevertheless, written statements of the principal facets of each job aid in keeping confusion to a minimum. In addition, written job descriptions, in the larger organization, aid in establishing a wage and salary structure. In allocating responsibilities and authority among senior subordinates, care should be taken to match these with their individual strengths and interests. It is a known fact that truly capable individuals will tend to shape their jobs to suit their capabilities, and management should take advantage of this tendency to its own benefit. At the same time, care must be taken to ensure that the various individual weaknesses which will always exist are adequately covered by the strengths of others.

There must be organization as soon as any enterprise expands beyond the proverbial "one-man show." Once constructed for a given set of circumstances and group of personalities, it must not be cast in concrete. People change, and circumstances change. A good manager keeps his organization flexible, and capable of being modified as necessary to suit prevailing conditions, without falling apart with every change in the wind.

2. BASE SALARY CONSIDERATIONS AND JOB EVALUATION

From the time one person first employed another, there has been a problem of how much to pay an employee. Today, the situation has not changed. There are two different forces which act on this problem. At times, their effects are difficult to reconcile.

The first force to be considered is that of supply and demand. Even though it assaults the ego of the individual worker, the fact is that labor as a group or class behaves as though it were a commodity in a free market. If demand for a particular skill and experience is high and the number of people available who possess the required skill and experience is low, rates paid will be abnormally high due to competition among employers. The reverse is also true.

The other factor is the development of the idea that some specific combinations of skills and experience have a distinct and possibly different relative value than others regardless of the level of ability or performance of any individual person who might be applying that combination. For example a skilled worker is generally considered to be more valuable than an unskilled one. This concept has an intrinsic appeal to most everyone.

The two foregoing factors appear to operate regardless of the level of ability and performance of any individuals occupying the job. Yet it is generally agreed that there are real differences in performance among different people, and that even though on the same job, they should be rewarded differently. This personal input on the part of the individual can cause differences in pay level, as will be discussed in Sections 3 and 4 of this chapter.

As soon as the organization becomes of size, perhaps twenty-five or thirty employees, this problem of setting salaries or wages can become sufficiently acute to require some form of organized, consistent manner for their establishment. One of the difficulties in the smaller organization is the separation of the requirements of the job itself from the personal contributions of the person who might be filling the job, regardless of whomever may be filling it at the moment.

As mentioned in the previous chapter, written job descriptions are of major assistance in clarifying organizational position, responsibility, and authority. They are equally useful as descriptions of the essential requirements of the job, no matter who happens to be filling it.

Placing a value on any job is as yet essentially subjective, and judgmental, and is dictated to some extent by supply and demand conditions. We can, however, make use of some aspects of scientific method to gain as much objectivity and consistency as possible in application despite the essentially subjective nature of the decisions made.

We can begin by looking at the existing situation. If we were to have a large waiting line of applicants for all types of positions, we could say with some justice that our existing wage structure probably is too high. If, conversely, we could not fill quite a number of diverse positions and many of our employees were leaving to take other positions, there is a distinct probability that the general wage structure is too low.

If neither of these extremes exists, we could assume with some degree of logic that the general wage structure was reasonable, although the probability is that it contains some wrongs, either over- or under-payment, which could be described as unreasonable departures from the general wage pattern.

The objective, here, would be to establish a general wage and salary structure "in the middle of the road," so that it will attract and hold employees, yet not be unreasonably costly. To accomplish this, it is necessary to maintain a clear distinction between the requirements of the job itself, regardless of the abilities or contributions of anyone currently filling it, and those personal contributions unique to the particular person filling the job.

To determine what is or is not an unreasonable departure from the general pattern of wages, it is necessary to determine that general pattern of wages itself in some quantitative form. This is best done by a process of formalized job evaluation.

The technique as developed toward the end of World War II was to select some factors by which various jobs could be compared, and which seemed to have a direct bearing on their relative value. These factors were:

1. SKILL

2. RESPONSIBILITY

3. EFFORT

4. JOB CONDITIONS

Most people will agree that differences between job requirements on any or all of these general factors should be recognized by differences in wages or salaries. However, these terms are somewhat fuzzy and undefined. What constitutes skill? Responsibility has many facets. Which of these facets has a bearing on the value of a job?

To clarify thinking, it was necessary to subdivide these general factors into more specific detailed factors which would lend themselves to clear definitions and bases for comparison. A widely used job evaluation system developed by the National Metal Trades Association uses the following factors.

Skill

Education (*Knowledge Required*)

Judged by specific items of knowledge required, and compared by the number of years of schooling and/or trade apprenticeship required to attain minimum acceptable performance.

Experience Required

Judged by the normal number of years of experience of a cumulative rather than repetitive nature required to attain minimum acceptable performance.

Initiative and Ingenuity (*Variety and Complexity*)

Judged by the number and complexity of problems to be solved by the employee at minimum acceptable level of performance, the requirements for self-starting and inventiveness by any employee on the job.

Responsibility

Responsibility for Product

Judged by the dollar effects on the enterprise judgmental errors on the part of an employee in the position affecting the product of the job.

Responsibility for Tools and Equipment

Judged by the dollar amount of average loss to the enterprise caused by errors by an employee in the position regarding equipment or tools used.

Responsibility for the Work of Others

Judged by the number of people whom an employee must direct or guide (such as more junior employees, or helpers) in performing the job.

Responsibility for Safety of Others

Judged by the extent of probable and possible harm to other employees or the public who are in the vicinity of the workplace.

Effort

Mental and Visual Effort

Judged by the amount of fine visual acuity required, together with the requirement for concentration and complex thought processes.

Physical Effort

Judged by the amount and frequency of physical effort required to attain minimum job performance.

Job Conditions

Surrounding Conditions

Judged in terms of the relative severity of surrounding conditions under which the job must be performed, and the frequency of exposure to them.

Hazards

Judged by the normal exposure to and seriousness of possible injury or to death.

Other things being equal, most people will agree that real differences between job requirements on any or all of these factors should be represented by differences in the wage to be paid for the job. For reasons which will appear, the judgment basis should be the requirements of the job as it would be performed at the minimum acceptable level.

Experience has shown that the ability of a group, or of people in general, to make judgmental decisions in a consistent fashion is limited to about five levels from low to high; low, intermediate low, middle, intermediate high, and high. Consequently, a scale of five levels or degrees from low to high is normally used, each with an appropriate point or numerical value running from low to high. Some practitioners tend to use a continuous scale from low to high such as 1 to 10 or 1 to 100 for each factor, in the interest of attempting to obtain greater refinement and accuracy. But there is some doubt as to the real efficacy of this attempt.

The evaluation should be undertaken by a group of supervisors under the guidance of an experienced professional who is aware of the various sources of error, and of the pitfalls which can interfere with sound evaluation.

The procedure normally used is to have each member of the group rate and compare each job with all the others on each factor several times, each time and each rating on a factor separated in time from the others, to minimize the effect of several sources of error which will be described in the following paragraphs.

One source of error in this type of segmented judgment-making process is called the "Halo" effect. A job which is rated particularly high or low on one factor will tend to influence the raters' judgments in the same direction on other factors, whether or not it is justified.

Another is the character and personality of the rater. There are optimists, pessimists, extremists, and many other types, more or less forceful and persuasive. Each may be more familiar with one group of jobs than another, and, may be unduly pursuasive, either high or low. The judgments of others in the group may be taken as a personal affront by such a person, to the detriment of objectivity.

Allowing some time delay between repeated ratings on each factor, plus effective leadership by the professional can aid in minimizing the effect of these errors and in obtaining effective results.

Interpreting the judgments in quantitative form requires discussion. It is generally agreed that the above rating factors are not of equal importance in making the pay judgment. It is generally agreed that skill is the major consideration, followed by responsibility, and that the other factors serve only to make reasonable distinctions between jobs where these major factors are substantially equal. A typical scale is shown below.

After degree ratings have been well tested and confirmed by at least three complete repetitions of the comparison process, the next step is to develop a picture of the existing wage or salary structure. With the preceding type of approach, the logical assumption is that there should be some sort of direct relationship between the point score awarded to

Exhibit 40

JOB EVALUATION SCALE					
FACTOR	DEGREE-POINTS				
	1	2	3	4	5
Knowledge	14	28	42	56	70
Experience	22	44	66	88	110
Initiative & Ingenuity	14	28	42	56	70
Responsibility for Equipment & Tools	5	10	15	20	25
Responsibility for Product	5	10	15	20	25
Responsibility for Work of Others	5	10	15	20	25
Responsibility for Safety of Others	5	10	15	20	25
Mental & Visual Demand	5	10	15	20	25
Physical Demand	10	20	30	40	50
Surrounding Conditions	10	20	30	40	50
Hazards	5	10	15	20	25
DEGREE-POINT TOTALS	100	200	300	400	500

the job by the job evaluation procedure, and the wage rate which should be paid for that job.

A simple way is to make a plot of job evaluation points for each job versus the wage paid to each employee on that job. The finished plot would look somewhat like Exhibit 42 following.

There is something about this picture which is quite different from those plots we have previously seen. The cloud of points is not a straight line, but bends upward with increasing point values. This seems very peculiar to many people. They expect that the relationship should be linear; that a job evaluation point should be worth the same monetary value no matter where it falls along the scale. This does not happen, however. In every case where there is a linear scale of points, this upward curve appears.

The true reason is not known precisely. However, a hypothesis has been advanced which might account for this phenomenon. This hypothesis draws an analogy with the physical ability to perceive differences.

If a person is blindfolded and given a 1-pound weight in one hand and a 2-pound weight in the other, he has no problem in making an immediate and correct distinction. If, however, the weights were 100 and 101 pounds respectively, it is unlikely that a correct decision as to

Exhibit 41

JOB EVALUATION
SUMMARY SHEET

JOB		FACTOR	KNOWL.	EXPER.	INIT. & INGEN.	RESP. EQUIP.	RESP. PROD.	RESP. WORK	RESP. SAFETY	MENT. & VISUAL	PHYS.	COND.	HAZARD	TOTAL
NO.	TITLE		Deg. / Pts.	Deg. / Pts.	Deg. / Pts.	Deg. / Pts.	Deg. / Pts.	Deg. / Pts.	Deg. / Pts.	Deg. / Pts.	Deg. / Pts.	Deg. / Pts.	Deg. / Pts.	PTS.

Robert N. Hoggatt

Exhibit 42

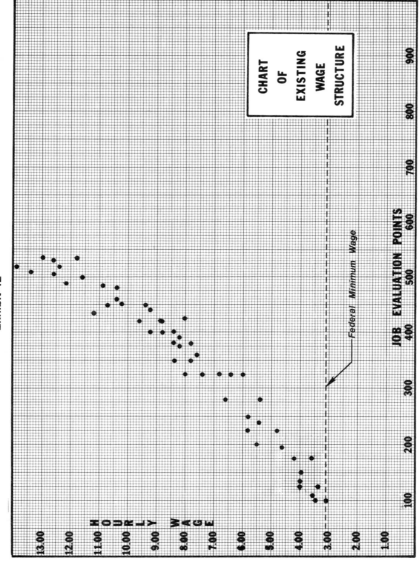

CHART
OF
EXISTING
WAGE
STRUCTURE

which was heavier would be made other than by chance. It seems, in this respect, that our ability to make distinctions is proportional to the weight or masses involved.

We can then make the analogy as follows. If we postulate that a complex job is "weightier" or has more "psychological mass" than a simple job, differences between "weighty" jobs would have to be larger to be distinguishable than would be the case with a simple job. Somehow, we seem to have done this over the many generations in which hiring and wage setting has taken place, and it seems to have been successful.

We hypothesized earlier that the general wage structure of the enterprise was generally correct. Now we need to develop a method of stating that general wage structure in quantitative terms. Again, the techniques of regression are available with which to determine the equation representing the existing average relationship between job evaluation points and money.

The equation we must develop is more complex, in order to take care of the element of curvature shown in the chart. Since the wage curve is usually of the growth or compound interest type, we can often get a good fit with the linear regression formula if we make use of logarithms of the x and y values in the computations. Or we can use parabolic regression instead of linear. These are explained in the Appendix, Section 1.

An Averge Relationship path has been calculated for the data previously plotted, and is shown in the following exhibit.

Earlier, while we agreed that the general wage structure as shown in the previous exhibit is probably reasonably correct, there is the possibility that there may be errors in the case of individual jobs or employees, either on the high or low side, and that errors are defined as unreasonable departures from the general wage pattern. Also, if one is to admit that differences in employee performance should be recognized by differences in pay, a range should be provided to make this possible unless there are measured work incentives in operation.

We can then define wage errors as payments outside of the ranges we propose to recognize as being reasonable for recognition of individual employee differences in performance.

The next question is how to determine what the boundaries of the range of reasonableness should be. An acceptable basis for making this determination might be to assume that the company's wage payments are reasonably close to right in approximately two-thirds of the cases, and wrong, either high or low, in the other one-third. This leads us to consider using the Standard Deviation around the trend line as an acceptable set of limits for this range.

There is one added consideration, which perhaps is not sound statistically, but is extremely practical. In order to have the same impact on employees, wage increases also need to be in proportion to the psychological weight or mass of the job. To accomplish this, it becomes necessary to have widening ranges as one ascends the scale of jobs. Therefore, a method of range determination using the Standard Deviation method of calculation is recommended, but with deviations calculated as percentages of the corresponding trend line value.

Exhibit 44 below applies this technique to the previous data. The technique, although perhaps not scientific, does gain credence from the recorded fact that as job evaluation ratings increase, one usually finds a corresponding increase in the width of scatter around any trend line found.

Exhibit 43

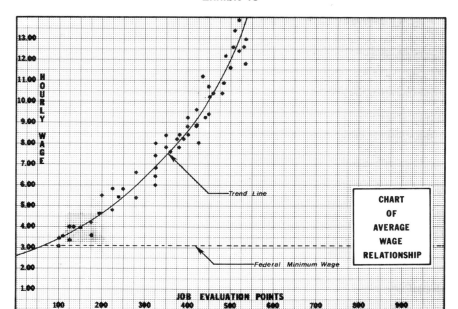

Exhibit 44

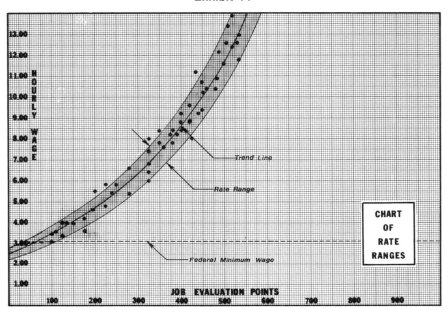

A continuous band of ranges may be perfectly all right for a very large organization with a great many jobs. However, since the evaluation process is still a judgmental one, some simplification might be in order. Also, promotion chains need examination to assure that the rate change which takes place upon promotion is significant in relation to the psychological mass of the jobs under consideration in that chain.

In scanning the usual plot of points versus wages, jobs often tend to cluster into larger groups, with gaps between them. These groupings can often be equalized and converted into grades, with point value boundaries such that there is a really distinct step up between one grade and the next. Such a grouping is shown in the following exhibit. Grade boundaries should either be even in point value, or gradually expanding with increasing point values. Arguments can be advanced for each.

In some large companies, there is no such grouping, and consequent inequities may be alleged on the close decisions regarding jobs which are close to grade boundary lines. There is no real help for this situation, except the possibility of adjusting job duties and re-evaluating so as to place such jobs clearly in one grade or another.

There is no sacred number of wage grades to be selected. It is a matter of convenience in administration, coupled with the idea of making a significant difference between one range and the next higher or lower. The simplification in administration comes about from the problem of maintaining the system in good order with the evolution of the business and job requirements that is a normal part of operation. With continuous ranges, any slight change in job content would require re-evaluation, and a minor change in rate. Under rate ranges, a change in job content must be great enough to change it from one grade range to another before other than cursory re-evaluation is necessary.

It should be noted here that rate ranges are only needed if there is no direct incentive pay plan in operation and employees' individual wage rates are to be established by performance appraisal (or "merit rating" as it is sometimes called) to establish the position of an individual employee within the rate range for the job.

Exhibit 45

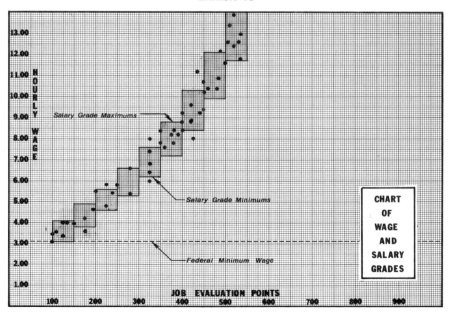

The philosophy of rate ranges is that any employee who can perform at least the minimum requirements of the job is worth at least the minimum rate for the job, while there is also an upper limit beyond which the job is not worth more, regardless of the abilities of any person who might fill it.

Upon installation of such a system, three classes of employees will be found; those who are paid less than the minimum rate for the job, those who are paid within the rate range, and those who are paid above the rate range. To adjust this situation demands some changes.

One could be factual, simply raise all underpaid employees to the job minimum and cut all overpaid employees to the level of their respective job maximums. The latter half of this proposal is unlikely to win any applause from employees, and can cause great resentment in the more capable of a company's employees; an undesirable situation.

An acceptable compromise has generally been to increase employees below minimum to their respective minimums immediately, on the basis that if they are not worth the minimum for their job, they should not be employed.

At the same time, since management has the major responsibility for permitting any overpayment, such employees should not be harmed. Instead, overpaid employees are not reduced, but "frozen" in place and are ineligible for further increases of any kind until either the general wage structure catches up with them through inflation, until their duties are increased to bring their new job into a rate range, or until they are promoted to another and higher rated job in a higher rate range and grade.

To assure remaining competitive in the job market, periodic wage surveys should be made to ensure that the company's wage structure is in line. Local chambers of commerce often conduct such surveys and can be of assistance in maintaining sound wage structures.

No firm policy can be offered for dealing with the occasional local shortage of some particular type of skill. If this skill is needed, a pay scale must be established for it such as will attract competent personnel, even from outside the area. If this creates an out-of-line situation, management must develop some type of compromise or temporary overpayment schedule for this situation to preserve the integrity of the remainder of the system.

Also, the above does not answer the potential problem of employees being paid within the established rate range, yet not being compensated in accordance with their contribution to the company. This aspect will be discussed in the following section.

3. INCENTIVE TECHNIQUES

In the small business area, there is a phenomenon which we label the "craftsman syndrome." This is a particular affliction of the person (usually of high personal or craft competence) who attempts to start and manage his own business in the area of his own expertise. His own competence makes it difficult for him to accept the lesser competence of other employees, and to gain his objective through the efforts of others rather than his own alone. The business fatality rate is particularly high for this type of person.

It is also very difficult for the individual proprietor or small business owner to realize the difference in motivation which exist between him and his employees. With the owner, the business often becomes the focal point for his existence, and its effective operation a matter of primary concern. Not so with the employee.

Usually, to the employee, a job is only a means to some other end; providing for himself and his family, going on vacations, permitting indulgence in hobbies and the like. If he loses his job, he seeks another. His loyalty to himself and his own interest takes precedence over any loyalty to or consideration of his employer in most cases. This is often difficult for the small business owner to understand, since his own overpowering concern for the business tends to blind him to this fact.

Because of this difference in concern, management must be constantly engaged in behavioral modification, and is constantly faced with the problem of controlling and directing on-the-job behavior of employees, in the face of their work often being a less than primary consideration to them.

The reward-punishment or "carrot and stick" technique is most frequent. In applying this technique in past times, emphasis was too often placed on the punishment aspect, where the employee worked under the constant threat of economic deprivation through loss of his job.

Little thought was given to the more positive aspects of encouragement and reward.

It has been well demonstrated that fear of punishment is a poor motivator with which to inspire superior effort or performance. Fear is the motivator of the slave, and was, perhaps more applicable in the days of slavery, when a slave was not called upon to use much intelligence or judgment.

Under today's more complex economy, overuse of fear as a major motivator tends only to inspire minimal and grudging performance, if not outright revolt. Obviously, any tendency toward employee revolt is not really in the best interest of the business. While it cannot be neglected, punishment probably should only be used as a measure of last resort.

Under present-day conditions, the matter of supplying positive motivation is a much more desirable path to pursue. The design of appropriate methods for doing this will vary with the type and level of job under consideration. For successful motivation, two essential characteristics should be present.

1. The reward for efforts should be prompt in timing, so the worker can relate his efforts to it directly.
2. The quantity of reward should be in direct proportion to the quantity of good work produced.

To varying degrees these principles are diluted in practice, and, to the extent of dilution, their motivational value is decreased. Four principal methods are in use.

1. Direct pay for production completed.
2. Indirect production-based bonuses.
3. "Merit" pay levels above job minimums.
4. Profit sharing.

There are three principal ways of paying for production completed; piecework, various standard-hour payment plans, and commissions on sales. Of these, piecework developed very early, and, in a sense, put the employee in business for himself, which could be considered a virtue. However, as production or the labor market changes, the rates also must change, which creates quite an administrative burden in time, effort, and cost. In addition, in the U.S.A. minimum wage legislation was passed on a pay per hour basis. Such legislation complicates administration and dilutes the full motivational value of piecework.

Standard-hour plans were devised to counter these administrative problems. In such plans, employees are assigned regular hourly rates, and then in line with previously discussed methods, standard times are assigned for each type of operation, and each good piece produced earns so many standard minutes for the employee, to be paid for at one-sixtieth of the employee's hourly rate for each standard minute produced. An average employee, under such a plan should earn 480 standard minutes in an eight-hour day. If he were to exert himself and produce at a faster rate, for example 600 standard minutes in an eight hour day, he would then receive ten hours of pay for eight hours of work.

Due to the influence of trade union collective bargaining in the U.S.A., most standard-hour plans now include a provision that an employee will receive no less than eight hours of pay for eight hours of work. This has a slight tendency to reduce motivation, since the downside risk to the poorly performing employee is eliminated. This, of course, eliminates some of the motivation from economic fear. In many cases under present conditions, this dilution is not serious.

Sales commissions, traditionally paid as a percentage of sales, are a special version of incentive or motivational pay for sales personnel. Otherwise, direct production incentives are usually applied only to those employees directly engaged in production. Sales employees, unfortunately, are motivated by the traditional commission arrangement merely to obtain a large volume of sales, without regard to the profit obtained. If management fails to control prices, the results can be a loss of profit.

Bonuses and group incentives are used to motivate indirect workers and lower echelon supervisors whose duties are not amenable to direct work measurement and standardization. As such, they can be used to pursue special management objectives, such as good housekeeping and safety, but do not have the direct motivational strength of the direct incentives.

So-called "merit" pay plans, particularly as applied to lower echelon employees, imply that at periodic intervals, employee performance will be reviewed, and a salary increase granted to above-average personnel. This is essentially a subjective technique, applied with varying degrees of rigor and formality, and subject to many abuses. It is most frequently applied to office, clerical, supervisory, and middle-management personnel whose duties are varied and not considered to be effectively measurable in quantitative terms.

When carefully used by well-trained and conscientious evaluators, and followed up by individual discussions with each employee to review results and to encourage specific improvements, this procedure can be quite successful. Being subjective, however, if mishandled its results can bring serious harm. Use of this technique should be approached with caution, and adopted only with careful and continuing supervision to minimize abuses.

The technique used is similar to that of job evaluation, in that a set of factors are developed by which, it is hoped, variations in employee performance and value can be judged. Supervisors familiar with the employee's performance and behavior do the rating. Serious flaws have often developed in applying this technique largely due to personality of the rater, and problems of psychology.

First, there is again the halo effect, as was mentioned in the previous chapter. Its effects are even more pronounced in employee appraisal than in job evaluation. Then there are differences among raters.

There is the eternal optimist: "I have a terrific bunch of people." There is the pessimist: "Gee what a bunch of clunks." There is the extremist: "I don't have any average people. My good people are terrific. My new people are hardly worth having." And there is the supervisor who can't or won't make any distinction: "Oh I guess they're pretty much average."

Again, there is a further hazard in the possibility for unwarranted favoritism toward particular employees on the part of the rater or raters. Little or nothing can be done about this, if the rater chooses to be persistent. One can only attempt to appeal to the sense of justice in attempting to train the raters.

Except for the problem of favoritism, the remaining problems can sometimes be aided by numerical manipulation; for example, one can assume that one person's concept of "an average employee" means just about the same level of performance as the same concept as rated by any other person. Rating employees by their standard deviation score (their deviation from the average score awarded by a particular rater) instead of by the raw score and pinning "average performance" to the midpoints of the rate ranges, helps to minimize some of the foregoing rater errors. This manipulative technique also aids in stabilizing wage rates, but it does not have scientific soundness, since no one can prove or disprove the idea of equality or the concept of "average" among raters.

Another approach is to try to eliminate these problems through a consensus of several raters. However, there is a serious problem in securing enough different raters to review an employee who are sufficiently familiar with the particular employee's performance to give a useful rating. Some assistance can be gained by seeking self-evaluation by employees, and reviewing them jointly with supervisory ratings.

There is benefit in reviewing results with the employee, provided it is done in an objective manner. However, unless done with exquisite care and dedication to objectivity on the part of all the raters, serious and extremely damaging backlashes can occur. Because of this, use of employee appraisal should be examined very carefully and cautiously before installation.

The profit-sharing approach has its best use at the upper management levels where profits are not only a matter of more direct concern, but where each participant has a more direct influence on the profits of the enterprise. Of the various types of management incentives, those oriented toward profit improvement are likely to be most useful in promoting the welfare of the enterprise.

In designing any profit-sharing plan, care must be taken to preserve the business. A reasonable dividend to stockholders, plus provision for some retained earnings to take care of needs for growth and replacement should be taken from after-tax profits before profit sharing among employees and management takes place.

4. JOB ENRICHMENT AND NONFINANCIAL MOTIVATION

One of the real benefits which can be obtained through a properly administered merit plan is the recognition and praise it affords to the individual employee. This "massaging of the ego" can have powerful and favorable results if founded on recognition of genuine merit. Lip service, however, is likely to result in a serious and harmful backlash.

In this respect, it could be just as well to avoid tying employee evaluation to pay, as mentioned in the previous chapter, and to use it as a means of developing and encouraging employees in a nonfinancial way.

Many hold the opinion that an employee is most happy and effective when his duties tax him fully and even push him a little, but do not seriously overtax him. Overtaxing, particularly in an emotional sense, is said to bring on discontent, failure, and even disease, such as hypertension and heart attacks. Underutilization of an employee's abilities can be equally damaging, however.

The overqualified and underutilized employee tends to become bored and discontented, which again breeds trouble for management, and wastes a valuable resource, except in cases where the employee's abilities are so completely underused that he can accomplish them by reflex and let his mind wander at will. Sometimes this particular situation can be endured without harming either the employee or the company, but this does not tend to maximize profits.

In areas of advanced production technology and automation, such as the U.S.A., requirements for intelligence, skill, and knowledge on the part of production employees are constantly being reduced, making people of lower and lower ability gainfully employable. In so doing, however, management is reaching further and further down from average in the bell-shaped normal curve of distribution into a constantly decreasing labor pool.

In consequence, in an expanding economy, the chances of an employee being underoccupied, particularly in the case of a heavily automated direct production job, are increased. The moderately underoccupied employee, then is the one who should benefit from efforts toward job redesign, under the various "job enrichment" plans such as that implemented by Volvo in Sweden.

There are a number of problems in attempting to implement such a program. Within the bounds of present organization formats as applied in production, the principal one is that of locating those employees to whom it would prove beneficial, and determining the extent of underemployment of each, so that some are not placed under excessive stress through overloading. Locating underemployed workers and properly diagnosing their needs and the extent of their underutilization can often require extensive use of professional psychological services which by nature are expensive.

The principal advances in such programs have been in the area of direct production. Similar programs for indirect, office, and clerical personnel lag behind. Job enrichment can be an expensive and time-consuming task, and it is still an open question as to the net real value of such programs.

Other nonfinancial or indirect means have been used with varying degrees of success in inspiring employee loyalty and "company spirit." Almost all of these activities are more or less paternalistic in nature. Sports activities, plus various forms of paternalism and employee welfare activities are the most frequent means. However, they can also be perceived as another aspect of "Big Brother" attempting to control all aspects of an employee's life, again, unfavorable toward the company. IBM is one of the companies more successful in using this form of motivation.

Of these types of motivators, health preservation activities such as insurance, clinics, and the like may be truly the most beneficial, but in recent years have become so widespread that they may have lost some of their motivational value. Also, with the recent changes in the value standards of the general public, measures which are perceived as paternalistic can have a negative effect.

It might seem, from recent experience with health care benefits, that the key to using nonfinancial rewards for motivational purposes may exist in having some flavor of uniqueness attached to it. Anything which is widely accepted and in use tends to lose its flavor and effectiveness as a motivator. Perhaps this comes about through loss of appeal to the instinct or desire of a person to be recognized as an individual, or at least to draw strength from membership in some special group which is recognized as being unique and desirable.

For whatever reason, it would appear that management should be prepared to advance new programs to replace those being widely copied and which show signs of losing effectiveness. The experience in using nonfinancial incentives ranges from extremely good to terrible. Consequently, the decision to use or not to use this avenue of motivation must remain with the individual manager, with no firm promise of success.

13. Marketing and Competition

1. BASIC QUESTIONS

We have not yet discussed one of the most important aspects of business operation, marketing. It is not enough to have a good product or service, or to be financially sound. People must buy the product or service in sufficient quantity to make the business viable and profitable.

In the case of the small shopkeeper, or the street vendor crying his wares aloud to the passerby may be sufficient. Often it is not. Almost certainly, any larger business cannot depend solely upon casual walk-in traffic if it is to prosper and grow, although many retail businesses do depend heavily on walk-in trade.

There is a series of questions which should be asked by anyone in or contemplating going into business, and which should be repeated at periodic intervals.

1. **Who, out there in the general public, wants or needs what I want to sell?**

2. **How many are there?**

3. **Of these, how many are ready and able to buy at any given time?**

4. **Of these, how many are now being served by others (Competitors!)?**

5. **What are these competitors doing?**

6. **Are there enough customers left to support my enterprise?**

7. **How can they find out about me and reach me?**

8. **How can I identify them?**

9. **How can I inform them of my existence and willingness to fill their needs?**

10. **What factors influence the number of real and potential customers at any particular time of the day, week, or year?**

11. **Do I really have the capacity to fill the needs and requirements of customers to their satisfaction?**

A good and useful product and service by themselves will not suffice to make a business. There must be customers, and there must be enough sales volume available to support a profitable enterprise, or failure is certain. Therefore, it is a good idea to do some market research to find out about the market before committing funds or effort into an enterprise. Failure to do enough market study before taking the plunge into business has been the downfall of altogether too many small businesses, and has contributed substantially to the extremely high mortality rate in small business.

In the case of an existing business, management cannot rest on its oars for long. Conditions change, the needs and tastes of the general public change, and management should always be prepared to shift plans, procedures, and products to move with that tide. Earlier we discussed the need for management to play the game of "What If" continually. Nowhere is this more important than in the area of marketing. Management, as with a stage performer or musician, must always be prepared for an encore in the form of a new or improved product or service.

To know that enough customers exist to support a business is not enough. There is no guarantee that they will buy. They must know of your availability, and must be able to make contact with you. To accomplish this requires thought, study, and effort, and can involve many different aspects, from design of signs and advertisements and selection of advertising media to arranging proper access and hours for business.

If you are in an existing business, what about competition? Is there any at present? What is the nature of the competition? If there is none, and the business is doing well, management should be particularly alert, for competition will soon develop.

People are still people, and when a person discovers that someone else has a good thing going, he usually wants to get a part of the action. Consequently, no monopoly can long endure in a truly free market. Even a patented item which becomes successful in the marketplace is soon imitated, and often infringed upon.

If a new enterprise is contemplated, what is the competitive situation? Are there others doing the same thing? If so, how much of the available market do they fill? If not, why not? Generally, if there is a market for a product or service, someone will find it sooner or later.

If the portion of the available market not satisfied by competitors is insufficient to support the intended enterprise, or if the existing market is already being satisfied by competitors, the only mode of entry is by taking existing business away from competitors. In this case, detailed knowledge of the competitors, their pricing, trade practices, policies, and state of customer satisfaction is vital to success.

Often such an attempt is perceived in the marketplace as inexperienced brashness, which adds to the problem of hewing one's way to a recognized viable market position. We will discuss ways of dealing with competition in the next section.

A major responsibility of management in maintaining a healthy business must always be a thorough familiarity with and understanding of its market. Whims, seasons, technology, fads, economic conditions, and the image of the enterprise in the minds of its customers all play a vital part in determining whether or not the enterprise will continue in good health.

Three other forces are now in operation much more strongly than in the past. These are exerting a progressively more serious influence on marketing efforts, even to the extent of having a major effect on the viability of the enterprise. These are:

1. **Concern with ecological protection.**

2. **Concerns for consumer welfare.**

3. **Concerns for employee health and safety.**

Many ecological concerns are legitimate and based in fact. Technology has been growing at an exponential rate resulting in some environmental effects which were not foreseen and consequently have caused damage to the environment and to public health. There have also been a few cases in which management paid no attention to the impact of their operations on the environment, surrounding inhabitants, or even their own workers. This is indeed a short-sighted variety of behavior.

Unfortunately, some well-intentioned and self-appointed leaders have gone overboard in their concerns about damage of the ecology, with consequent unnecessary legislative intervention and overkill, resulting in unreasonably high cost impact on business. Very often, in the real world as it now exists, trade-offs must be made between environmental concerns and the ability of civilization and business to exist on its present level. There is a serious need to strike a fair balance in whatever trade-offs must be made. In the small business sector, with limited financial means, the impact of injudicious legislation can be extremely severe.

In the past, the customer was held to be intelligent and capable of making sound choices in his purchases. The doctrine of "Caveat Emptor" or "Let the Buyer Beware!" was supported by the courts, placing on the consumer the obligation to take care of his own welfare. He bought at his own risk. This situation has completely turned about in recent years.

Today, the situation is one of "Caveat Vendor" or "Let the Seller Beware!" In the past, there have been cases of fraud upon customers, and of customers being damaged economically and even physically by faulty products or products sold by means of misleading or even fraudulent advertising. This has given color and impetus to the efforts of self-appointed activist leaders to create changes in this situation. Often, in their zeal, these people go overboard and become unrealistic in their requirements.

Courts have extended the doctrine of implied merchantability, required extensive clarification of warranty language, and have made clear the obligation of those who would sell to the public to deliver an honest and safely functional product or service. Over-reaction has occurred. This obligation in some cases has been extended to the retail level, making retailers responsible for products or services which they did not create, and over which they have no control except to stop selling the product.

In so doing, the courts have opened the way to as much falsification and cheating on the part of customers as previously may have existed on the part of some vendors, and perhaps more, again punishing the many for the sins of the few. This is of particular concern to the smaller vendor, whose financial resources are limited.

The same thing has happened to the protection of the employee. Historically there were cases of inadequate concern for the health and safety of workers. This behavior is not good business in the long term, since a trained worker is an asset and represents an investment in the cost of training which can only be recovered by use of his services in production. A sick or injured worker, incapable of working, represents a temporary or even permanent loss of this investment.

Nevertheless, sufficient cases occurred to arouse the activists, and again the legislatures and courts over-reacted, with the result that an effective trade-off has not yet been found. This again is of serious concern to the smaller enterprise with limited resources with which to resist the overzealous bureaucrat or activist who becomes unrealistic in his demands.

Even more important than the direct financial cost of compliance with the legal requirements stemming from this general antibusiness atmosphere, is the effect on sales of even unfounded allegations of environmental damage, poor or falsely advertised products, or carelessness of employee health and safety. Not too many years ago, the cranberry industry in New England was nearly wiped out by false allegations concerning the insecticides used.

These are components of the present business environment in which management must operate, and they have substantial impact on the format, direction, and impact of sales efforts, and on the reception of the product or service in the marketplace. Their extent and probable future direction are necessarily of major concern.

Again, management must continually look toward the future. Decisions on production, facilities, employment, training, finance, and almost every other aspect of operations are future oriented. And all of them depend on sound estimates of the future ability to sell the company's products or services. Sales forecasting and other forms of economic forecasting are discussed in a later chapter.

2. MARKET RESEARCH FOR SMALL BUSINESS

Market research, in the mind of the average person in or contemplating entering business for himself, is an arcane subject only discussed in the recesses of universities and used only by the very biggest companies with huge resources. Nothing can be further from the truth. Anyone can do market research. The basic need is to realize the need for it, to determine what information is needed, and to have the courage and energy to go and find out.

Many of the research techniques are available and can be used by anyone. The individual must only take a little time to think through and define his problem, and do a little studying on methods of interpretation. The first thing to realize is that a great many people are willing to answer questions if asked. Secondly, there is a great deal of statistical information available for someone who knows where to look and is willing to make the effort.

A prime resource is the U.S. Census reports which are available in almost any public library. Area or local chambers of commerce are often of great help. A major purpose of trade associations is the collection and publication of useful statistics, often related to census data. There are many others.

The principal problem is determining what questions to ask. Some serious thought must be given to the framing of the detailed questions to be asked of the general public to supply satisfactory answers to the basic questions set forth in the previous chapter.

Questions must be clear. They must be carefully phrased to avoid misinterpretation. They must be simple. They must be retested several times against the question, "What am I really trying to find out?" And above all, they must be asked of the general public. One must indeed go and find out.

There are several ways of finding out which anyone can use.

1. House-to-House Canvassing. All you need is your list of questions, a plan, and a good pair of legs.

2. Telephone Surveys. Here, you need a telephone, but do not need legs. The rate of response will be lower.

3. Mail Surveys. This does not take much physical effort, but can be costly in postage and the production cost of the mailed question-naire. The rate of return of answers is likely to be much lower. 1% to 3% is considered very good, so a lot of mailing must be done to get enough answers to be meaningful.

4. Questioning Random Passers-by at One or More Locations. This is useful in special cases where the business is local, and perhaps is dependent on the amount of traffic passing by.

There are some tricks about each of these surveys that are useful to know. The time of day the survey is taken can be important. If one has some idea of the characteristics of the typical customer, or has some particular type or class of customer as a target market, one needs to select a time when he is most likely to talk with a member of this class or type.

If one does not know the characteristics of the typical customer, it is good to find out in advance, so the survey can be most useful. If the product or service has been in existence, there are probably statistics which can be found or developed from trade association and/or census data which will describe such a customer.

If the customer is likely to be a member of some particular economic or ethnic class or group, the survey questions need to be in language suitable to be understood by that class or type of person, and the survey should be concentrated if possible in areas inhabited by that class or group. Often the best type of question is one which can be answered by a simple yes or no.

Next is the determination of how many answers are needed to supply an adequate description of the situation. This can be answered by a little study of statistics to determine sample size. This is a bit more complex than it sounds, but we have already been dealing extensively with statistics and probability, and sampling is just one further step.

When we speak of sampling, we are again using probability, on the assumption that the sample will closely resemble the entire population under consideration. When we sample, there always exists the possibility that the sample taken will not have a good enough resemblance to the population, and that consequently, we can expect some sampling error. We must first decide how much sampling error we will tolerate before determining how large a sample we will need.

Naturally, the larger the sample size, the more closely it is likely to resemble the population itself. However, any survey has cost attached to it; printing, planning, the actual cost of labor of making the survey, and the labor cost of interpretation. There is a sort of break-even point of compromise between the cost of surveying, and the level of accuracy obtained, which must be studied in each case.

The statistical calculations involved in determining an appropriate sample size can be complex and difficult. A useful assumption for precision is to have a 95% chance of being correct, with a level of precision, varying both plus and minus, from 1 to 5%. The following table shows the appropriate sample size for these levels of precision.

One can see from this table that obtaining very high reliability (99%) and precision (+/−2% or less) can become very costly in terms of the size and cost of the sample to be taken and analyzed. In most cases, such precision is unnecessary.

In the case of the smaller business, there may not be even enough time to make enough contracts to furnish a statistically sound sample. Nonetheless, provided that the surveyor does not permit himself or

Exhibit 46

SAMPLE SIZES		
PRECISION	**RELIABILITY**	
	95% SAMPLE SIZE	99% SAMPLE SIZE
±5%	400	1,200
±4%	625	2,500
±3%	1,111	4,444
±2%	2,500	10,000
±1%	10,000	40,000

herself to indulge in wishful thinking, he can get a relatively sound idea of his market situation.

To repeat, the most important thing about market research is to DO IT!

Anyone can, and it is inexpensive insurance to reduce the gamble of beginning and maintaining business.

3. TRENDS OVER TIME

Whether or not changes should be made in the operation is a matter of constant concern to any manager. Guidance as to what kind of changes to make, and in what direction, is not necessarily furnished by the reports of the spot situation at the end of an accounting period, such as a month or a year.

As we have said, all management decisions are of necessity future oriented, and to make them, we must look for trends or patterns of past behavior, and if they are found, make the assumption that they are likely to repeat.

What is happening to the various key ratios over time is a matter of necessary concern to determine what the trend might be. If the trend is favorable, perhaps no changes will be needed. If the direction of the trend is unfavorable, then, certainly, the manager should consider taking some action to institute some type of change in his plan of operation.

It is often helpful to the manager to see a graph or picture of the past behavior of these ratios, of sales, of profits, and of many other similar figures over some extended period of time. At times, by seeing such pictures, a trend is immediately apparent. At other times, the data fluctuates too much for a trend to become apparent to the unaided eye. In this case, the data must be worked over so as to average out the fluctuations into a smooth trend, and to make the trend visible, so it can be used for predictive purposes.

Numerous mathematical methods are available with which to accomplish the development of a smooth trend. Among these are:

1. Moving averages

2. Linear and nonlinear regression

3. Exponential Smoothing

Although discussion of the operational mathematics of application of regression methods and of exponential smoothing has been placed in Section 4 of the Appendix for reference, and we have discussed other applications for regression in previous chapters, it will be useful at this point to discuss the details of application of each of these techniques.

There is much more to forecasting than mere establishment of a trend. There is always the possibility of seasonalities, and of other cycles as well. We must attempt to determine these quantitatively as well as making a measured statement of the degree of variability or uncertainty around that trend with the effects of seasonality and cycles included if we wish to do as sound a job of forecasting as possible.

It is always of value to see a picture in addition to columns of numbers. Consequently graphing is useful. A good graph may let us see whether there is any regularized up and down movement, or cycles in the data, whether seasonal or otherwise.

Also, by spreading or condensing the scale of one axis or the other, we can often see trends more clearly, even without the mathematics.

If the general trend has been established, we can have some expectation that it will continue for some unknown distance into the future. We cannot be absolutely certain of this, hence we need some kind of statement of the degree of uncertainty which exists in the past data, on the assumption that at least this degree of uncertainty will apply to the projection into the future.

As an example, we show above a table of the month-by-month sales of a company which we have seen previously. Looking at the data, it is very difficult to see if there is any trend.

Now we shall chart it. As you can see, a line connecting the monthly points is jagged and uneven, and it is difficult to see a trend. Yet, if we were managing this company, we certainly would want to make some kind of projection.

Exhibit 47

MONTH	SALES		MONTH	SALES
SALES				
COMPANY A				
1.	11,300		10.	10,325
2.	13,460		11.	12,672
3.	9,750		12.	9,680
4.	8,560		13.	8,750
5.	9,300		14.	9,635
6.	10,425		15.	10,140
7.	14,675		16.	12,835
8.	13,460		17.	14,247
9.	11,223		18.	15,620

Exhibit 48

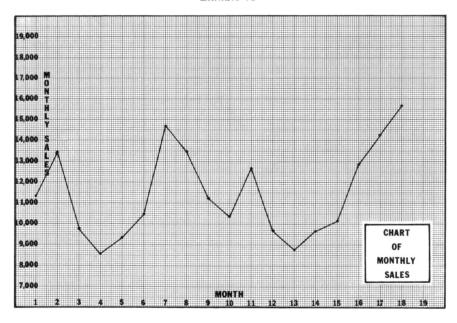

Calculation of moving averages tends to damp out some of the variation. The technique is simple to use. One begins by averaging a consecutive group of months, and plotting that value for the last month in the group. For the plot of the next month, we delete the earliest month from the data, add the latest month, and reaverage. This process is repeated for all the data to be used. Naturally, the larger the block of data used to construct the average, the more damping occurs, and the more any cycles and variations disappear. This can be highly deceptive at times when precision of forecasts of the immediate future are desired.

We have calculated a three-month moving average for the company, which results in the somewhat smoother graph shown below.

Use of various methods of regression tends to yield more accurate results as to trend, without damping out the individual points, which still might reveal a cyclical activity around the basic trend. We have developed a linear trend line through this data, which we show below.

This trend line, because of the mathematical regression process by which it was developed, is the most accurate averaging line (at its own degree of complexity) that can be developed. One can see, however, that the individual data points are scattered at various distances from the trend line. This usually represents the operation of random factors impossible to predict, the existence of some type of cyclical activity, or a combination of both.

The trend line shown is linear. More often the trend is one of growth at an increasing or percentage rate similar to the compound interest growth curve which has been discussed previously. This requires linear regression using logarithms or parabolic regression as discussed in Section 1 of the Appendix. The simplest curve which can be developed (either linear or compound interest growth) will furnish us with a basis for predicting the probable future variation, and the chances of its occurrence.

To interject greater precision where any set of cyclical or other complex activity is involved, more complex regression curves can be developed by increasing the size and complexity of the equation which represents the curve of relationship. The mathematical computations become quite burdensome as the complexity of the curve equation increases. A decrease in this computational requirement may be accomplished by using the method of orthogonal polynomial regression, also shown in Section 3 of the Appendix.

Exhibit 49

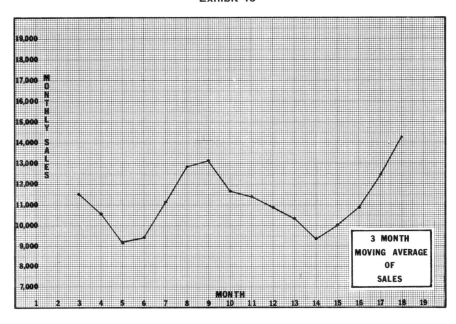

Exhibit 50

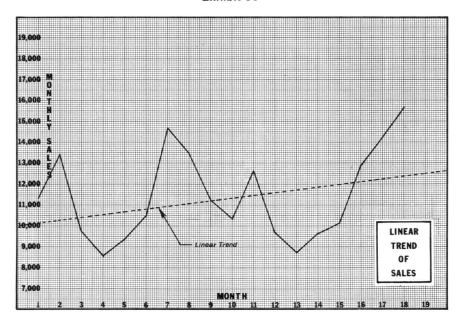

Exponential smoothing is another method of increasing the precision of short-range forecasting, taking advantage of being able to deal with any cycles which may be present. This method works with and smooths out patterns of departure above and below a basic trend line. It operates in a self-adjusting fashion with changes in history as they emerge. A discussion on the use of this method is included in the Appendix. As is noted there, however, applicability of this method is largely limited to forecasting the next period only.

In all our discussion to this point, we have dealt with figures as though the dollar were of a constant real value. Factually, this is not true. In depressed times, such as in the 1930s, a dollar was hard to get, prices were low, and the real value of the dollar was high in terms of its power to purchase goods and services.

In more recent times, we have been experiencing a long-term period of inflation, and a steady decline in the real purchasing power of the dollar. The effects of changes in purchasing power of the dollar need to be removed, so that business, in particular may know whether or not it is experiencing real growth.

The Federal government publishes regular reports on the cost of living, and its rates of inflation or deflation. To reach a constant dollar level measurement of activity, a dollar value must be selected for some past year, which is taken as the base year, and the values of subsequent years either discounted, successively for periods of inflation, or compounded upward to compensate for periods of deflation below the base value. Detailed information on the history and trend of inflation is shown in Section 5 of this chapter.

Considerations of inflation or deflation trend should and must be a definite part of financial planning and of the evaluation of an investment of any type until such time as the trend of continuing inflation is stopped or reversed, since inflation and deflation also influence the present value of moneys to be received in the future. For example, in present value determinations during inflationary periods, the probable inflation must be added as an additional discount factor reducing the value of future income, in addition to other investment criteria, if real buying power is to be maintained.

4. DEALING WITH COMPETITION

As was mentioned in the previous section, competition will almost certainly be found to exist, or will soon develop. There are three general ways of dealing with competition.

1. Ignoring its existence.

2. Meeting it head on.

3. Eliminating its effectiveness.

Ignoring competition is extremely dangerous, although occasionally, some well-established, complacent enterprise falls into this error, and eventually finds itself with no business.

Meeting competition head on is one potential way of eliminating its effectiveness, but it can be a bloody encounter. Competition of this type can and often does involve price cutting, sometimes to the point of extinguishing profits, or one-upmanship in advertising and/or service to customers, which by increasing costs of operation soon has the same effect. This type of war can only be won by the enterprise with the greatest depth of resources. The survivor of such a war may recoup losses later, through the elimination of competition, but this is not a permanent situation, and sooner or later will require repetition. In addition to the potential harm from head-on-head price wars, it is possible under certain conditions to buy out competition.

However a large warning notice must be posted regarding use of the bloodier tactics to eliminate the effects of competition, even though the aggressor might have sufficient resources to win the battle. Our free economy concept rests upon the need to maintain free and "fair" competition in the marketplace, and in pursuit of filling that need, we have developed a substantial ethical and legal structure acting against "unfair competition," and blatant cases of "unfair competition" are frequently pursued for redress through the courts.

A way to eliminate competition is to buy it up. This, however, is often beyond the means of the person in the smaller businesses, and in addition may be subject to the legal strictures mentioned above.

The most effective means of competition is to remove its effectiveness by means of the creation of an image of uniqueness of your enterprise or product in the mind of the general public, which, whether true or not, tends to create a factual monopoly, thereby eliminating effective competition.

The creation of an image of uniqueness is not done easily, and it may be somewhat costly. However, it is usually less costly than a price war, and leaves the enterprise in the position of being pursued by would-be competitors, instead of pursuing them. This is a definitely more satisfactory, although transient condition.

However, to maintain it can be burdensome. When pursuing this strategy, management, more than ever must play the game of "What if," and constantly be prepared with alternatives and innovations to maintain its strategic and tactical lead. An example is the pattern of competition in the fast-food (hamburger) business between MacDonald's, Burger King, and Wendy's. Previously, the pattern of fast foods was the hot dog vendor, and the sandwich shop with a diversified menu.

MacDonald's began by developing a highly standardized single product and a method of producing it at minimum cost. For a time it enjoyed phenomenal growth. Soon, the others followed. Now we see MacDonald's expanding their menu to include beverages and sundaes. Again the others follow, each attempting to maintain an image of specialization and uniqueness; Wendy's with its chili, and Burger King with added advertising. Now MacDonald's has expanded further to the "steak burger"; a new product. One day in the not too distant future, we shall probably see these specialized operations expanded into full line restaurants, and then the cycle of competition in specialized products will begin all over again.

Price is always a weapon in dealing with competition, but it is a two-edged sword, cutting both ways. As was mentioned earlier, it is a far better tactic to do a superior job of controlling costs, so as to supply an extra margin for dealing with competitors who might be tempted to begin price competition.

In an earlier chapter, we mentioned that cutting Variable costs is the best way of improving the competitive position and profitability of a business, as compared with reduction of Management costs, or increasing prices. This choice rests on several considerations. First, in a competitive situation, cost reduction is more desirable than price increases because a price increase invites the would-be customer to shop elsewhere. Secondly, a percentage reduction in Management costs results in only a similar percentage decrease in the company's break-even point.

However, a percentage reduction in variable cost leverages itself and may result in almost a two to one percentage of reduction in break-even point, depending on the percentage relationship of Variable Cost to Sales. Exhibit 51 shows how this happens and may be used as a guide.

The reader will notice that the effect on the break-even point of percentage decreases in Variable Cost becomes greater and greater with decline in the company's Contribution Ratio, or with increase in the percentage of Sales represented by Variable cost.

Consideration must also be given to the effects of changes in the purchasing power of the dollar, evidenced in recent years by constant inflation, and decline of the purchasing power of that monetary unit. History and trends of behavior of inflation, and strategies for dealing

Exhibit 51

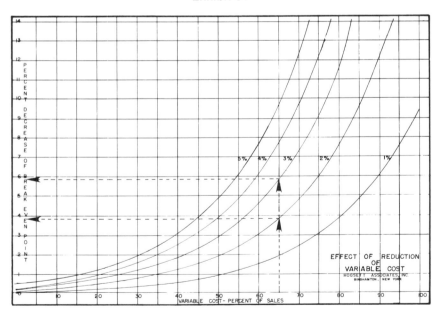

with its effects of changing the value of the dollar, will be discussed in the following section.

5. DEALING WITH INFLATION

Much of our conventional everyday thinking on financial matters is on the basis of a constant monetary value; that the dollar does not change in value with the passage of time.

Unfortunately, the fact is that the dollar has changed in its power to purchase real wealth, and is doing so continually. We have experienced a prolonged period of inflation which has tended to invalidate not only the figures of five years ago, but even last year's data.

This tends to make sound forecasting difficult, and it becomes even more difficult when inflation operates at double-digit levels as it sometimes has, to see if a business is truly growing, or even keeping pace with inflation or deflation. It is necessary, then, to know the rate of inflation and of the decline or change in the purchasing power of the dollar, and to include such changes in the day-to-day plans for business operation.

In fact, inflation has become such an accepted part of economic life that for many years its effects have been ignored. Today, it has accumulated to a level at which even the smallest additional increment becomes very significant.

The person in small business can no longer afford to ignore its effects, and must take positive efforts to deal with it to his own benefit.

Investors have the same problem. Companies publish their earnings and costs at regular intervals, and investors often reach their judgments by making comparisons of a company's performance from one year to the next.

Despite monetary controls by the Federal Reserve system, and apparently without much influence by whichever political party has attained the Presidency of the Country, (although the Democratic party has controlled Congress since 1940 for all intents and purposes), not only has inflation of some degree been in operation for 38 of the last 40 years, but the annual rate of inflation itself as reflected in the Consumer Price Index has shown a trend of constant increase with the passage of time. (See Exhibits 51 and 52.)

The Federal government publishes statistics which give the cost of living, each month. The real effects of inflation tend to be hidden by the way the statements are made; that is, the statements give the percent of inflation over the previous month, not giving much recognition to the way this really grows over several years.

The following table lists annual inflation from January 1940 through December 1979, together with the value of a 1939 dollar year by year during that same period.

For example, 1979 showed a 13% annual rate of inflation. Therefore, a business must have incresed its profits in dollars by 13% for 1979 from the profits of 1978 merely to have the same real purchasing power

Exhibit 52

INFLATION HISTORY							
YEAR	ANNUAL RATE	ACCUMULATED INFLATION	1939 $1	YEAR	ANNUAL RATE	ACCUMULATED INFLATION	1939 $1
1940	0.96	100.96	.99	1960	1.60	213.53	.47
1941	5.00	106.01	.94	1961	1.01	215.69	.46
1942	10.66	117.31	.85	1962	1.11	218.08	.46
1943	6.15	124.52	.80	1963	1.21	220.72	.45
1944	1.74	126.69	.79	1964	1.31	223.61	.45
1945	2.28	129.58	.77	1965	1.72	227.46	.44
1946	8.53	140.63	.71	1966	2.86	233.97	.43
1947	14.36	160.82	.62	1967	2.88	240.71	.42
1948	7.77	173.32	.58	1968	4.20	250.82	.40
1949	(.97)	171.64	.58	1969	5.38	264.32	.38
1950	.98	173.63	.58	1970	5.93	279.99	.36
1951	7.90	187.34	.53	1971	4.30	292.03	.34
1952	2.18	191.42	.52	1972	3.30	301.67	.33
1953	.75	192.86	.52	1973	6.23	320.46	.31
1954	.50	193.08	.52	1974	10.97	355.61	.28
1955	(.38)	193.08	.53	1975	6.5	378.73	.25
1956	1.49	195.96	.51	1976	5.80	400.70	.25
1957	3.56	202.94	.49	1977	6.50	426.75	.23
1958	2.73	208.48	.48	1978	9.00	465.16	.21
1959	.81	210.17	.48	1979	13.00	525.65	.19

as in 1978. Many people in small business fail to realize the full effects of inflation, merely realizing that their costs are rising, and that they must do something about them. Development of suitable tactics for use by the person in small business will require some fine-tuned financial planning to which most are not accustomed.

If figures for several years are used, they should be adjusted to a constant dollar value by means of the following equation, expanded as necessary to cover the time period involved.

Adjustment to Constant Dollar

Where:

r_{aN} = Annual Inflation Rate for Year N
RV = Real value adjusted for inflation from Year 0
PV = Present Value Without Adjustment

Equation 26: $$RV = \frac{PV}{(1 + r_{a1}) \times (1 + r_{a2}) \times (1 + r_{a3}) \, x \ldots x \, (1 + r_{aN})}$$

A business operator must look to the future if his business is to continue. We have projected what will happen if history continues as it has in the past.

Three trends were extracted from this history:

1. Trend of Annual Inflation Rates

2. Trend of Accumulated Inflation

3. Trend of Accumulated Inflation, 1970 fwd.

The results are set forth in the table on the following page.

In computation we have developed only the long-term trends, and have ignored the very severe surge since 1976. If that short-term trend continues, the United States will very soon be confronted with the disaster of valueless money. Prevention of this catastrophe is still possible, but the possibility decreases with each day the inflation continues.

As we can see, if only the long-term trends continue, by the year 2000 our poor 1939 dollar will be worth somewhere around $.05. This is indeed a dismal prospect for life insurance owners, people on fixed incomes, and for owners of all of our retirement and other "dollar stable" investments.

Inflation has progressed at an average rate of 4.1049% per year compounded continuously since 1940. That is to say, to have a 1939 dollar maintain its buying power as of January 1, 1980, a person would have needed the equivalent of placing $1 on January 1, 1940 in a savings account paying an annual rate of 4.1049% compounded continuously.

If this rate of compounding were to be continued, by the year 2000 inflation would be 1256.14% of the 1939 level, and the 1939 dollar would have shrunk to $.0796; not far from the indications of the other trends.

We can well ask what the prospects may be for a change in direction. They are probably poor. Individuals can do very little, except to try to

Exhibit 53

	THE POSSIBLE FUTURE						
Y E A R	TREND 1 Annual Rate			TREND 2 Accumulated		TREND 3 Accumulated,1970...	
	Rate	If Accumulate	1939 $1	Percent	1939 $1	Percent	1939 $1
1980	5.53	573.25	.17	549.21	.18	559.87	.18
1981	5.59	605.31	.17	591.68	.17	603.84	.17
1982	5.65	639.53	.16	637.53	.16	651.29	.15
1983	5.71	676.06	.15	686.91	.15	702.45	.14
1984	5.77	715.08	.14	739.94	.14	757.64	.13
1985	5.83	767.36	.13	796.36	.13	817.16	.12
1986	5.89	812.56	.12	857.52	.12	881.35	.11
1987	5.95	860.90	.12	922.33	.11	950.59	.11
1988	6.01	912.63	.11	991.34	.10	1,025.27	.10
1989	6.07	968.01	.10	1,064.68	.09	1,105.81	.09
1990	6.13	1,027.32	.10	1,142.49	.09	1,192.68	.08
1991	6.19	1,090.87	.09	1,224.90	.08	1,286.38	.08
1992	6.25	1,159.00	.09	1,312.05	.08	1,387.44	.07
1993	6.30	1,232.07	.08	1,404.07	.07	1,496.44	.07
1994	6.36	1,310.48	.08	1,501.09	.07	1,614.00	.06
1995	6.42	1,394.66	.07	1,603.25	.06	1,740.79	.06
1996	6.48	1,485.07	.07	1,710.70	.06	1,877.55	.05
1997	6.54	1,582.22	.06	1,823.55	.05	2,025.05	.05
1998	6.60	1,686.69	.06	1,941.94	.05	2,184.13	.05
1999	6.66	1,799.04	.06	2,066.02	.05	2,355.72	.04
2000	6.72	1,919.94	.05	2,195.91	.05	2,540.78	.04

reduce their own costs in every way possible before raising prices. Collectively, however, we must realize the true causes of inflation, for only by collective action can we change the trend.

There are a great many influential people who have a vested interest in continuing inflation. With inflation, labor leaders can continue demanding increases, and the government gets more taxes so that politicians can cement their positions by sociological and welfare handouts. Others in business say that this is better than the alternatives. We have even heard some prominent economists say "A little inflation is good for growth."

One could inquire, "Whose growth?" for the real effect of inflationary behavior is to punish the frugal who develop savings and are the source for the lenders of capital, to destroy the capital base upon which growth develops, and to erode the value of many of the social benefits for which its operation was proposed to pay.

It is nothing more than a deliberate fraud perpetrated upon the taxpaying public, and upon those individuals, both business and private, who are prudent and frugal.

The alternatives are unattractive to many, and they are politically unacceptable to those with vested interests in continued inflation, among whom are the politicians whose decisions, laws, and programs have done so much to stimulate it.

Halting or reversing this inflationary trend will indeed require some bad tasting medicine for many people. The medicine may include such things as forbidding the federal or state governments to operate at a deficit, making substantial changes in the income tax laws involving some sort of indexing for adjustment to changing values of the dollar, accepting an unemployment rate dictated by employment market conditions, elimination of the minimum wage, and removal of governmental interference with the collective bargaining process in all forms.

This will require the strongest sort of sober, controlled collective pressure on all levels of government, particularly the federal level, for here lies the principal responsibility for the excessive spending, debt formation, and economically unsound laws and practices which have produced the situation.

The alternative to controlled readjustment of inflation causing conditions could well be uncoordinated panic and "pulling in the economic horns" as in the 1929 crash, resulting in another severe de-

Exhibit 54

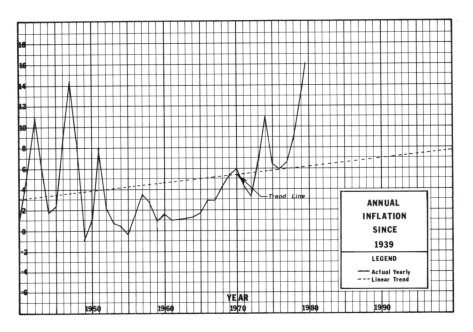

pression before equilibrium is restored. We have already seen the early signs. Bankers are being very restrictive in lending policy, interest rates are at an all-time high, squeezing the small business operator and the general public, and contributing to the ascending spiral of costs and prices.

It seems unlikely that any turn-around will occur during most of 1980, for it is an election year, and legislators have already demonstrated that they are not about to change their vote-buying habits, and the general public so far seems to be oblivious to continuing to have its pocket picked.

The person in small business does not have sufficient individual economic power to stabilize the situation. He must, therefore attempt to deal with the day-to-day situation as best he can. This is probably best done by anticipating inflation with an attempt at precision, and acting accordingly.

Two areas of major concern need to be considered. If the present trend continues and inflation continues to accelerate, the loss of value

Exhibit 55

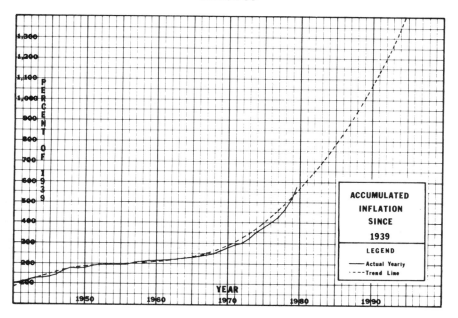

of accounts receivable with the passage of time becomes greater, and it becomes more and more important to avoid sales for credit.

Also, unless there is a substantial corrective change in governmental policy, a crash becomes more and more inevitable as the brute force of economic necessity and generalized lack of public optimism toward future prospects takes over. When this happens, the ability to repay credit previously extended in times of optimism is seriously impaired, resulting in another force to push the economy downhill at an accelerating rate.

At the same time, the erosion of inventory values by accumulation of holding costs through the passage of time is counteracted by inflation, so that increasing inventory and inventory holding time to some extent can become attractive. This, however, requires additional investment, often necessitating borrowing by the small business, at high interest rates.

Unfortunately, due to competition in the marketplace, uncontrollable costs for small business tend to rise before prices, so that the small

Exhibit 56

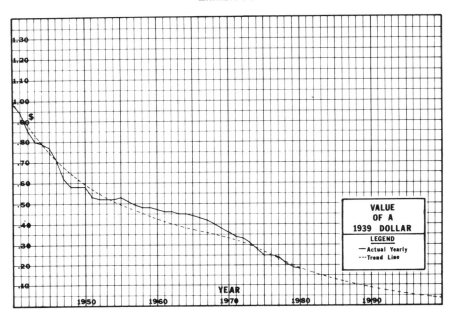

business is squeezed. This places even more emphasis on the need for the manager of a small business to be alert to make every possible reduction in the costs which he can control.

To illustrate the effect of cost reductions, a reduction of 1% in management costs will also reduce the company's break-even point by 1%. More importantly, however, as we saw in Exhibit 50 depending upon the gross profit ratio, a similar 1% reduction of variable cost, usually achieved through reduction of waste and improvement of worker productivity will result in anywhere from a 1% to as much as 6 or 7% (in a low-margin business) increase in competitive margin in sales.

When inflation occurs, just to stay even in purchasing power, each year's sales and profits must increase. For example, for a 1980 sales target to stay even would be (1979 × 1.0554). To adjust for annual inflation, multiply the figures for the previous year by one plus the annual inflation rate expressed as a decimal.

The percentage change from the previous month can be converted into an annual rate by means of the following procedure.

Accumulated Inflation, Monthly

Where:

r = annual percentage change as a decimal.

$\dfrac{r}{12}$ = monthly percentage change as a decimal.

Equation 27: $r = (1 + r_{m1}) * (1 + r_{m2}) * \ldots * (1 + r_{m12}) - 1.00$

With the cumulative effect of inflation over several years in terms of change from a base year, this becomes:

Accumulated Inflation, Annual

Where: c = Cumulative change from Base Year as a decimal.
r_{aN} = Annual rate of each year as a decimal.

Equation 28:

$$c = (1 + r_{a1}) * (1 + r_{a2}) * \ldots * (1 + r_{aN})$$

In each case, if percentages are desired, multiply the results by 100. You will notice that this is another example of compounded interest which we discussed earlier.

If deflation should take place in some particular month or year under consideration, that particular term becomes:

$$\frac{1}{(1 + r_{aN})}$$

Unfortunately, inflation has become an accepted way of life for many people, to the point where its effects have been ignored until recently. Today, it has accumulated to the point where even the smallest increment becomes very significant. The person in small business can no longer afford to ignore its effects and must take positive action to deal with it to preserve himself and his business.

Inflation operates just like compound interest on a savings account, except in reverse. It is a compounding LOSS! The amount lost in any one period of time is relatively insignificant, but the accumulation over a number of years is horrible.

The answer for the person in small business lies in a combination of the following strategies.

1. Eliminate cost in every way.
2. Do everything possible to increase productivity.
3. Minimize credit sales.
4. Pursue collections vigorously.
5. Leverage prudently by selective borrowing.
6. Increase inventory carefully on popular items. *Just in time*
7. Study your market carefully and keep prices in line.
8. Maintain a high degree of alertness for changes in trends, and for a possible reversal.
9. Do not borrow so heavily that an economic reversal would cause too heavy a debt load.
10. Buy inventory prudently, with knowledge of holding costs. Do not lock up too much cash, but expand inventory selectively.
11. Be prepared to change course rapidly in event of a sudden downturn.
12. If in manufacturing, control the inventory of finished goods carefully for fast turnover.
13. Buy and expand inventories of raw materials carefully and prudently.
14. Do not convert raw materials or build finished goods inventory without confirmed orders unless the item is proven to be depression proof.
15. Maintain contact with the chamber of commerce, and particularly with the small business council, if there is one, to assist with their lobbying efforts to modify inflationary laws and practices.

Free bread and circuses for the people, governmentally fostered inflation, overspending, and progressive devaluation of the currency has been the downfall of every civilized nation since antiquity. If we are not to follow history, there must be a change in that mode of operation. That variety of "free lunch" is far too expensive. We cannot afford it and remain a viable nation, or a viable civilization.

Since writing the preceding comments, we have had a national election. The results have shown clearly that at long last the general public has awakened to the real situation. It now remains to be seen if it is not already too late; if indeed the damage can be repaired before the full crash. The alternatives are fearful beyond description.

14. Conclusion

1. Summary

We have discussed many ways of diagnosing business problems, and have suggested numerous remedies, all in the interest of maintaining a business in good health. In the interest of brevity, we have not dealt in detail with many of the techniques discussed, nor have we gone through all the scholarly proof which would normally be included in a textbook.

There are many excellent texts on the market which thoroughly detail statistics, managerial accounting, market research, decision theory, and the other aspects of management science which have been touched here only in passing.

The principal thrust of this effort has been to show some of the ways available to management, particularly those engaged in smaller enterprises, to obtain more definitive information about their own operations, and about their business environment, and to persuade managements to make better and more extensive use of these ways. If this effort is successful in attaining that end, not only will the individual business become more prosperous, but the country as well, for no country today can prosper unless supported by a sound base of strong, viable business, both small and large.

For those who might wish to have assistance, or to inquire further into application of these techniques to their own particular business situation, aid is available. Inquiries can be directed to the nearest college or university school of business administration, the U.S. Small Business Administration, state departments of commerce and industry, or even to the author.

Small business, as diffused and chaotic as it may seem, is still the bedrock of support for the remainder of the economy of the United States, and indeed, of the world. Small business entrepreneurs are the source of much of the effective innovation and technological development upon which our continuing civilization depends.

Yet the demands upon the owner-manager are becoming increasingly severe, and his margin for error is shrinking into insignificance.

We cannot let ourselves fall behind or fail because we cannot keep up with conditions. Being highly individualistic it is difficult for us as individuals to surrender enough of that individuality to band together around common problems and interests for mutual benefit and exercise of the economic and political force equivalent to our true economic value.

In the past, that force has been dissipated by our own individualism, and has been used against us in a sort of "divide and rule" technique. Individually and collectively we have suffered, and the nation is less strong as well. While diversity is the strength of small business, and of the nation, we must recognize our common concerns and needs, and have the strength to merge our diversity in pursuit of the welfare of the country.

To paraphrase a former president of General Motors: **WHAT IS GOOD FOR SMALL BUSINESS WILL PROSPER THE NATION.**

Appendix

1. LINEAR REGRESSION METHODS

Regression is a way of determining the quantitative relationship between two interdependent variables, and of determining also the extent of their interdependency. Use of the techniques of regression produces an equation which relates the two variables in a quantitative fashion, and guarantees that the relationship is more accurately stated than by any other equation of similar complexity which could be developed.

It is not the purpose here to write a treatise on statistics, or to engage in any intellectual exercises of proof of the principles given. This may be obtained from any standard college text on statistics. The purpose here is to demonstrate the use of regression as a tool by which to gain information for management in sufficient procedural detail so that it can be used for this purpose.

In all of the situations given in the various parts of the preceding text, the reader deals with the inter-relationship of two variables. Although regression methods may be applied to a multivariable problem, this type of problem goes beyond the realm of the average person in business and demands the aid of a professional in most circumstances. We shall deal here with the two-variable situation.

In dealing with such a relationship, one variable may be described as independent, or capable of being selected arbitrarily. The second variable then becomes dependent, with its value being determined by the equation of relationship once a value for the independent variable has been selected.

In this book, the independent variable has been labeled x and the dependent variable has been labeled y. In plotting graphs, which is an excellent way of determining whether there is any relationship between two variables, x (the independent variable) is usually plotted along the horizontal axis, and y, the dependent variable, along the vertical axis.

In Chapter 4, Section 3, in which the Cost-Profit-Volume relationship was discussed, this plotting technique was used to look for patterns of relationship. In this case, Sales was used as the independent variable x (since it is uncertain, and can be selected arbitrarily at need) and Profit (or Loss) was selected as the dependent variable y, since we have already agreed that profit usually varies with the amount sold.

The first key to using this general technique is to make a plot of the two variables, plotting a dot for each combination of x and y, and seeing whether or not there is a visible pattern or orderly arrangement to the resulting dots. The emergence of any fairly visible pattern to the arrangement of dots is a sure indication that the two variables are mathematically related in some fashion. The mathematical procedures below are designed to state that mathematical relationship in precise terms.

At times, due to scatter, which we have also discussed, a pattern will not be easily visible, as was seen in the case of the sales trend, and the trend of annual inflation rate which has previously been discussed. Then the techniques of regression and correlation will disclose the extent of relationship, if any.

The simplest form of an equation of relationship is that of a straight line.

Equation of a Straight Line

Where:

y = The Dependent variable
x = The Independent or controlling variable
a = A constant peculiar to the relationship
b = A second constant peculiar to the relationship

Equation 29:

$$y = a + bx$$

The mathematical problem is then to determine appropriate values for a and b such that they best describe the average relationship between x and y. To do this, two items are required.

1. The introduction of one other figure N which is the number of pairs of x and y values being studied.
2. Preparation of some statistics from the x and y values, which is done on a work sheet form such as that shown below.

Fill in the data on the work sheet in the following manner.

1. Enter each x and y.
2. Multiply each x by itself and enter the result in the x^2 column on the same line.

Exhibit 57

| x = _____ | WORK SHEET | | | |
| y = _____ | LINEAR REGRESSION | | Date: | |

N	x	y	x^2	xy
1				
2				
3				
4				
5				
6				
7				
8				
9				
10				
11				
12				
13				
14				
15				
16				
17				
18				
19				
20				
21				
22				
23				
24				
25				
26				
27				
28				
29				
30				
31				
32				
33				
34				
35				
36				
37				
38				
39				
40				
41				
42				
43				
44				
45				
46				
47				
48				
49				
50				
Totals $\sum$				

Robert N. Hogsett

3. Multiply each x by the corresponding y and enter the result in the xy column on the same line.
4. Total each column and enter result where called for. (Column Totals are denoted $S[x]$, $S[y]$, etc.)

The four column totals, denoted by $S(x)$, $S(y)$, etc., together with the number of x and y pairs (N) will be used to determine the values for a and b in the equation of average relationship.

 a and b are related by the following simultaneous equations, which, when solved for a and b will give values for the equation of best fit.

Simultaneous Equations

Equation 30:

$$aN + bS(x) = S(y)$$
$$aS(x) + bS(x^2) = S(xy)$$

Solving these equations is done as follows.

Determination of *b*

Equation 31:

$$b = \frac{S(xy) - \left\{\dfrac{S(x)S(y)}{N}\right\}}{S(x^2) - \left\{\dfrac{S(x)S(x)}{N}\right\}}$$

Determination of *a*

Equation 32:

$$a = \frac{S(y)}{N} - b\left\{\frac{S(x)}{N}\right\}$$

The a and b thus found are the constants for the straight line which will best fit the data.

 a is labeled the "Intercept," which is the value for y when $x = 0$. In the Profit Chart (Cost-Profit-Volume Relationships, Exhibit 9) the intercept is the level of the apparent Management Cost.

b is labeled the "Slope" which is the rate of change of *y* for a 1-unit change in *x*. In the Profit Chart, this is the Contribution Ratio.

Attention should be given to the various signs in the regression equation. Solution by ordinary algebraic rules will supply the correct signs for any set of data. A + sign for *a* indicates that *y* has a positive value when $x = 0$. If the sign is negative (−), *a* has a negative value. If the sign for *b* is +, the line moves upward as *x* increases, and the line moves downward if the sign for *b* is negative (−).

Similar rules hold for more complex regression equations, which will be discussed in following sections of the Appendix.

2. COMPLEX REGRESSION

There are some cases where growth, compound interest, and similar items show a curved pattern rather than a straight line. This curve can often be "straightened out" by plotting it on logarithmic graph paper rather than the quadrille ruled type. Semi-Log and Log-Log papers are available in many stationery stores. Semi-log papers have a logarithmically divided axis one way, and an equally divided one the other way.

If a straight-line pattern shows up on Semi-Log paper, convert the values of that variable to their corresponding common logarithms and substitute the log values in the appropriate columns in the work sheet. Carry out the calculations of *xy*, etc., using the log values instead of the original values.

If a straight-line pattern only appears on Log-Log paper, where both axes are logarithmic, then both *X* and *Y* values must be converted into their corresponding logarithms before proceeding to the work sheet. Then fill out the work sheet using the log values instead of the original values.

Two other ways are available for calculating equation values to fit curving data.

1. The equation of the straight line can be expanded to greater complexity.

2. The method of Orthogonal Polynomials can be used.

In a more complex regression, the next level is the parabolic curve.

Parabolic Curve

Equation 33: $y = a + bx + cx^2$

In this equation c represents the rate of change of b for a one unit change in x (the element of curvature).

If the sign of c is $+$, the line bends upward with increasing x, and if $-$, the reverse, curving downward.

The simultaneous equations governing the determination of a, b, and c are as follows.

Simultaneous Equation Set

Equation 34:
$$aN \quad + bS(x) \ + cS(x^2) = S(y)$$
$$aS(x) \ + bS(x^2) + cS(x^3) = S(xy)$$
$$aS(x^2) + bS(x^3) + cS(x^4) = S(x^2y)$$

The rules of simultaneous equations require that there be as many equations as there are unknowns (in this case, 3), and that each equation contain all the unknowns. A comparison of the arrangement of the straight line equation and the parabolic equation reveals a pattern which can be used to develop equation sets for more variables ($d, e, f . . .$). Ascending powers of x are used. For example, adding the constant d to the equation of relationship, would cause it to take the following form.

Third Degree Curve

Equation 35: $y = a + bx + cx^2 + dx^3$

The following would need to be added to the preceding equation set.

$$\underline{\quad} \quad \underline{\quad} \quad \underline{\quad} + dS(x^3) = \underline{\quad}$$
$$\underline{\quad} \quad \underline{\quad} \quad \underline{\quad} + dS(x^4) = \underline{\quad}$$
$$\underline{\quad} \quad \underline{\quad} \quad \underline{\quad} + dS(x^5) = \underline{\quad}$$
$$a(x^3) \ + bS(x^4) + cS(x^5) \ + dS(x^6) = S(x^3y)$$

In each case, the work sheet would require additional columns to contain the additional values required by the expanded equation sets.

A solution work sheet format for a parabolic curve is shown as Exhibit 58 on the following page.

A caution should be entered here. The labor of computation for more complex curves becomes great, and is rarely needed for business purposes.

Exhibit 58

SOLUTION WORK SHEET
PARABOLIC REGRESSION

Line	a	b	c	k	Instructions
1	N	$\Sigma(x)$	$\Sigma(x^2)$	$\Sigma(y)$	Enter from Work Sheet
2	-1				Divide each item (a,b,c,k) line 1 by -N (-a, line 1) and enter in same columns.
3	$\Sigma(x)$	$\Sigma(x^2)$	$\Sigma(x^3)$	$\Sigma(xy)$	Enter from Work Sheet
4					Multiply each item of line 1 by item b, line 2 and enter in same columns.
5	0				Sum each item on line 4 and same item, line 3.
6	0	-1			Divide each item on line 5 by -item b, line 5.
7	$\Sigma(x^2)$	$\Sigma(x^3)$	$\Sigma(x^4)$	$\Sigma(x^2y)$	Enter from Work Sheet
8					Multiply each item of line 1 by item c, line 2 and enter in same columns.
9	0	0			Multiply each item of line 6 by the algebraic sum of item b, lines 7 and 8.
10	0	0			Sum each item, lines 7, 8, and 9.
11	0	0	-1		Divide each item by -item c, line 10. Result is the final value for c. Enter as item c, line 14.
12					Multiply item c, line 14 by item c, line 6, change sign and sum with item k, line 6. Enter as item b, 14
13					Multiply item b, line 2 by item b, line 14 and item c, line 2 by item c, line 14, change both signs and sum with item k, line 2. Enter as item a, line 14.
14					

FINAL VALUES

Robert N. Hogsett

Exhibit 59

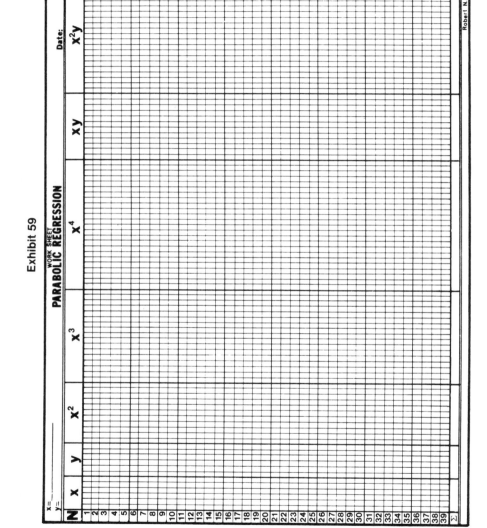

Economists and natural scientists use curves of greater complexity, and often have access to computers to supply the labor. The person in small business often does not need such complexity.

3. ORTHOGONAL POLYNOMIAL REGRESSION

For occasions where more complex curves of regression are needed, the method of Orthogonal Polynomials, although having a very formidable sound, becomes very useful in reducing the volume of computations for solutions. The real effect of this method is to shift the vertical axis to the right from its normal position, into the center of the data, so that values of the independent variable must be redetermined, and will take on both negative and positive values. As redetermined, we shall label the independent variable t. An additional column must be added to the worksheet form for the value t, given by the following equations.

EQUATION FOR t_0

Equation 36:

$$t_0 = \frac{S(N)}{N}$$

EQUATION FOR t

Equation 37:

$$t = x - t_0$$

The general form of the equation of relationship is as follows. Note that one can begin with a straight line, and progressively add more coefficients as desired, without the need to recalculate values for lower level coefficients.

Orthogonal Polynomial Trend

Equation 38:
$$y = a + bt + ct^2 + dt^3 + et^4 + ft^5$$

The data work sheet will change format. A format follows.

Exhibit 60

DATA WORK SHEET

ORTHOGONAL POLYNOMIAL REGRESSION

N	X	Y	T	TY	T^2Y	T^3Y	T^4Y	T^5Y
1								
2								
3								
4								
5								
6								
7								
8								
9								
10								
11								
12								
13								
14								
15								
16								
17								
18								
19								
20								
21								
22								
23								
24								
25								
26								
27								
28								
29								
30								
31								
32								
33								
34								
35								
36								
37								
38								
39								
40								
Σ								

Robert N. Hoggatt

The following group of equations governs the values of the constants a, b, c, etc.

Orthogonal Polynomial Coefficients

Equation 39: $a = \dfrac{S(y)}{N}$

Equation 40: $b = \dfrac{12}{N(N^2 - 1)}\, S(ty)$

Equation 41: $c = \dfrac{180}{N(N^2 - 1)(N^2 - 4)}\left\{ S(t^2 y) - \dfrac{N^2 - 1}{12} \right\} S(y)$

Equation 42: $d = \dfrac{2800}{N(N^2 - 1)(N^2 - 4)(N^2 - 9)}\left\{ S(t^3 y) - \dfrac{3N^2 - 7}{20*}\, S(ty) \right\}$

Equation 43: $e = \dfrac{44100}{N(N^2 - 1)(N^2 - 4)(N^2 - 9)(N^2 - 16)}\left\{ S(t^4 y) \right.$

$\left. - \dfrac{3N^2 - 13}{14}\, S(t^2 y) + \dfrac{3(N^2 - 1)(N^2 - 9)}{560}\, S(y) \right\}$

Equation 44: $f = \dfrac{698544}{N(N^2 - 1)(N^2 - 4)(N^2 - 9)(N^2 - 16)(N^2 - 25)}\left\{ S(t^5 y) \right.$

$\left. - \dfrac{5(N^2 - 7)}{18}\, S(t^3 y) + \dfrac{15N^4 - 230N^2 + 407}{1008}\, S(ty) \right\}$

The principal value of Orthogonal Polynomial Regression may well be short-range forecasting, in which the trend is complex.

The principal usefulness of the Orthogonal Polynomial method is that the values of the constants (a, b, c, etc.) do not change with addition of elements. In contrast to complex regression, with Polynomials the value of a, once determined, remains the same whether the equation is a simple straight line, or a complex curve. As a result, if added complexity is desired, only the values for the additional constants need be calculated.

4. EXPONENTIAL SMOOTHING

As mentioned in Chapter 13, Section 3, "Trends Over Time," Exponential Smoothing is another way of obtaining forecasts. While other methods, such as moving averages and regression require the carrying forward of a considerable amount of historical data, this is not true of Exponential Smoothing. Only three pieces of information are required to operate this technique.

1. The most recent past forecast.

2. Actual demand for that period.

3. A smoothing constant, arbitrarily selected, ranging between 0 and 1.

The value of the smoothing constant determines the sensitivity of reaction of future forecasts to past variations between forecast and actual demand. A company with a well-established and stable pattern of sales would use a low value for the smoothing constant, such as .05. Conversely, a company with a highly volatile sales situation would want a more prompt and effective reaction to a variation from plan, and would use a higher value for the smoothing constant, such as .30.

The basic forecasting technique operates in accord with the following equation for a single forecast.

Exponential Smoothing

Where:

F_n = Forecast for next period
F_{n-1} = Forecast for most recent previous period
A_{n-1} = Actual results for most recent previous period
p = Smoothing constant

Equation 45: $F_n = F_{n-1} + p(F_{n-1} - A_{n-1})$

If extended over several forecasting periods, the results tend to track more accurately as the reaction sets in. When this is done the results take the form shown below.

Extended Exponential Smoothing

Where:

F_0 = First forecast

Equation 46: $F_n = [A_{n-1} + (1 - p)A_{n-2} + (1 - p)^2 A_{n-3} + (1 - p)^3 A_{n-4} +$

$$(1 - p)^4 A_{n-5} + \ldots + (1 - p)^{n-1} A_0] + (1 - p)^n F_0$$

In using the exponential smoothing technique, it should be noted that the result is a reactive one, and will probably not forecast with extreme precision. Since it reacts and adjusts to past performance, forecasts will lag behind the direction of future events, particularly if a reversal of trend occurs. This may tend to inhibit its usefulness in certain situations.

5. CORRELATION

The Coefficient of Correlation is a very useful means of expressing the degree of relationship or association between two variables. It ranges from -1.00 (indicating a perfect inverse relationship between the variables), through 0 (indicating no relationship between the variables), to $+1.00$ (indicating a perfect direct relationship between the variables). It is determined by the following equation.

Coefficient of Correlation

Where:

r = Coefficient of Correlation
y = Original values for y corresponding to x value
y' = Trend line of y for same value of x
$S(\ )$ = Sum of (Value in brackets)
N = Number of pairs of x and y values

Equation 47: $r = \sqrt{1 - \dfrac{S(y - y')^2}{S\left\{y - \dfrac{S(y)}{N}\right\}^2}}$

The extent to which the resulting Coefficient differs from 1.00 is a measure of the exterior influence of other factors than the independent variable.

Exhibit 61

TABLE OF AREAS UNDER THE NORMAL CURVE

D/SD	.00	.01	.02	.03	.04	.05	.06	.07	.08	.09
0.0	.0000	.0040	.0080	.0120	.0159	.0199	.0239	.0279	.0319	.0359
0.1	.0398	.0438	.0478	.0517	.0557	.0596	.0636	.0675	.0714	.0753
0.2	.0793	.0832	.0871	.0910	.0948	.0987	.1026	.1064	.1103	.1141
0.3	.1179	.1217	.1255	.1293	.1331	.1368	.1406	.1443	.1480	.1517
0.4	.1554	.1591	.1628	.1664	.1700	.1736	.1772	.1808	.1844	.1879
0.5	.1915	.1950	.1985	.2019	.2054	.2088	.2123	.2157	.2190	.2224
0.6	.2257	.2291	.2324	.2357	.2389	.2422	.2454	.2486	.2518	.2549
0.7	.2580	.2612	.2642	.2673	.2704	.2734	.2764	.2794	.2823	.2852
0.8	.2881	.2910	.2939	.2967	.2995	.3023	.3051	.3078	.3106	.3233
0.9	.3159	.3186	.3212	.3238	.3264	.3289	.3315	.3340	.3365	.3389
1.0	.3413	.3438	.3461	.3485	.3508	.3531	.3554	.3577	.3599	.3621
1.1	.3643	.3665	.3686	.3718	.3729	.3749	.3770	3790	.3810	.3830
1.2	.3849	.3869	.3888	.3907	.3925	.3944	.3962	.3980	.3997	.4015
1.3	.4032	.4049	.4066	.4083	.4099	.4115	.4131	.4147	.4162	.4177
1.4	.4192	.4207	.4222	.4236	.4251	.4265	.4279	.4292	.4306	.4319
1.5	.4332	.4345	.4357	.4370	.4382	.4394	.4406	.4418	.4430	.4441
1.6	.4452	.4463	.4474	.4485	.4495	.4505	.4515	.4525	.4535	.4545
1.7	.4554	.4564	.4573	.4582	.4591	.4599	.4608	.4616	.4625	.4633
1.8	.4641	.4649	.4656	.4664	.4671	.4678	.4686	.4693	.4699	.4706
1.9	.4713	.4719	.4726	.4732	.4738	.4744	.4750	.4756	.4762	.4767
2.0	.4773	.4778	.4783	.4788	.4793	.4798	.4803	.4808	.4812	.4817
2.1	.4821	.4826	.4830	.4834	.4838	4842	.4846	.4850	.4854	.4857
2.2	.4861	.4865	.4868	.4871	.4875	.4878	.4881	.4884	.4887	.4890
2.3	.4893	.4896	.4898	.4901	.4904	.4906	.4909	.4911	.4913	.4916
2.4	.4918	.4920	.4922	.4925	.4927	.4929	.4931	.4932	.4934	.4936
2.5	.4938	.4940	.4941	.4943	.4945	.4946	.4948	.4949	.4951	.4952
2.6	.4953	.4955	.4956	.4957	.4959	.4960	.4961	.4962	.4963	.4964
2.7	.4965	.4966	.4967	.4968	.4969	.4970	.4971	.4972	.4973	.4974
2.8	.4974	.4975	.4976	.4977	.4977	.4978	.4979	.4980	.4980	.4981
2.9	.4981	.4982	.4983	.4984	.4984	.4984	.4985	.4985	.4986	.4986
3.0	.4986	.4987	.4987	.4988	.4988	.4988	.4989	.4989	.4989	.4990
3.2	.4990	.4991	.4991	.4991	.4992	.4992	.4992	.4992	.4993	.4993
3.3	.49952									
3.4	.49966									
3.5	.49977									
3.6	.49984									
3.7	.49989									
3.8	.49993									
3.9	.49995									
4.0	.49997									

Exhibit 62

PRESENT VALUE OF $1

DUE AT THE END OF Y YEARS

AT ANNUAL INTEREST RATES OF 1% TO 15%

Year	1%	2%	3%	4%	5%	6%	7%	8%	9%	10%	11%	12%	13%	14%	15%
1.	.99010	.98039	.97007	.96154	.95238	.94340	.93458	.92593	.91743	.90909	.90090	.89286	.88496	.87719	.86957
2.	.98030	.96117	.94260	.92456	.90703	.89000	.87344	.85734	.84168	.82645	.81162	.79719	.78315	.76947	.75614
3.	.97059	.94232	.91514	.88900	.86384	.83962	.81630	.79383	.77218	.75131	.73119	.71178	.69305	.64797	.65752
4.	.96098	.92385	.88849	.85480	.82270	.79209	.76290	.73503	.70843	.68301	.65873	.63552	.61332	.59208	.57175
5.	.95147	.90573	.86261	.82193	.78353	.74726	.71299	.68058	.64993	.62092	.59345	.56743	.54276	.51937	.49718
6.	.94204	.88797	.83748	.79031	.74622	.70496	.66634	.60317	.59627	.56447	.53464	.50663	.48032	.45559	.43233
7.	.93272	.87056	.81309	.75992	.71068	.66506	.62275	.58349	.54703	.51316	.48166	.45235	.42506	.39964	.35383
8.	.92348	.85349	.78941	.73069	.67684	.62741	.58201	.54027	.50187	.46651	.43393	.40388	.37616	.35056	.32690
9.	.91434	.83675	.76642	.70259	.64461	.59190	.54393	.50025	.46043	.42410	.39092	.36061	.33288	.30751	.28426
10.	.90529	.82035	.74409	.67556	.61391	.55839	.50835	.46319	.42241	.38554	.35218	.32197	.29459	.26974	.24718
11.	.89632	.80426	.72242	.64958	.58468	.52679	.47509	.42888	.38753	.35049	.31728	.28748	.26070	.23662	.21494
12.	.88745	.78849	.70138	.62460	.55684	.49697	.44401	.39711	.35553	.31863	.28584	.25667	.23071	.20756	.18691
13.	.87866	.77303	.68095	.60057	.53032	.46884	.41496	.36770	.32618	.28966	.25751	.22917	.20416	.18207	.16253
14.	.86996	.75787	.66112	.57747	.50507	.44230	.38782	.34046	.29925	.26333	.23199	.20462	.18068	.15971	.14133
15.	.86135	.74301	.64186	.55526	.48102	.41726	.36245	.31524	.27454	.23939	.20900	.18270	.15989	.14010	.12289
16.	.85282	.72845	.62317	.53391	.45811	.39365	.33873	.29189	.25187	.21763	.18829	.16312	.14150	.12289	.10686
17.	.84438	.71416	.60502	.51337	.43630	.37136	.31657	.27027	.23107	.19784	.16963	.14564	.12522	.10780	.09293
18.	.83602	.70016	.58739	.49363	.41552	.35034	.29586	.25025	.21199	.17986	.15282	.13004	.11081	.09456	.08080
19.	.82774	.68643	.57029	.47464	.39573	.33051	.27651	.23171	.19449	.16351	.13768	.11611	.09806	.08295	.07026
20.	.81954	.67297	.55367	.45639	.37689	.31180	.25842	.21455	.17843	.14864	.12403	.10367	.08678	.07276	.06110
21.	.81143	.65978	.53755	.43883	.35894	.29415	.24151	.19866	.16370	.13513	.11174	.09256	.07680	.06383	.05313
22.	.80340	.64684	.52189	.42195	.34185	.27750	.22571	.18394	.15018	.12285	.10067	.08264	.06796	.05599	.04620
23.	.79544	.63416	.50669	.40573	.32557	.26180	.21095	.17031	.13778	.11168	.09069	.07379	.06014	.04911	.04017
24.	.78757	.62172	.49193	.39012	.31007	.24698	.19715	.15770	.12640	.10153	.08170	.06588	.05322	.04308	.03493
25.	.77977	.60953	.47760	.37512	.29530	.23300	.18425	.14602	.11597	.09230	.07361	.05882	.04710	.03779	.03038

Exhibit 63

PRESENT VALUE OF $1

DUE AT THE END OF Y YEARS

AT ANNUAL INTEREST RATES OF 16% TO 30%

Year	16%	17%	18%	19%	20%	21%	22%	23%	24%	25%	26%	27%	28%	29%	30%
1.	.86207	.85470	.84716	.84034	.83333	.82645	.81967	.81301	.80645	.08000	.79365	.78740	.78125	.77519	.76923
2.	.74316	.73051	.71818	.70616	.69444	.68301	.67186	.66098	.65036	.64000	.62988	.62000	.61035	.60093	.59172
3.	.64066	.62437	.60863	.59342	.57870	.56447	.55071	.53738	.52449	.51200	.49991	.48819	.47684	.46583	.45517
4.	.55229	.53365	.51579	.49867	.48225	.46651	.45140	.43690	.42297	.40906	.39675	.38440	.37253	.36111	.35013
5.	.47611	.45611	.43711	.41905	.40188	.38554	.37000	.35520	.34111	.32768	.31488	.30268	.29104	.27993	.26933
6.	.41044	.38984	.37043	.35214	.33490	.31863	.30328	.28878	.27509	.26214	.24991	.23833	.22737	.21700	.20718
7.	.35383	.33320	.31392	.29592	.27908	.26333	.24859	.23478	.22184	.20972	.19834	.18766	.17764	.16822	.15937
8.	.30503	.28478	.26604	.24867	.23257	.21763	.20376	.19088	.17891	.16777	.15741	.14776	.13878	.13040	.12259
9.	.26295	.24340	.22546	.20897	.19381	.17986	.16702	.15519	.14428	.13422	.12493	.11635	.10842	.10109	.09430
10	.22668	.20804	.19106	.17560	.16151	.14864	.13690	.12617	.11635	.10737	.09915	.09161	.08470	.07836	.07254
11.	.19542	.17781	.16192	.14756	.13459	.12285	.11221	.10258	.09383	.08590	.07869	.07214	.06617	.06075	.05580
12.	.16846	.15197	.13722	.12400	.11216	.10153	.09198	.08339	.07567	.06872	.06245	.05680	.05170	.04709	.04292
13.	.14523	.12989	.11629	.10420	.09346	.08391	.07539	.06780	.06103	.05498	.04957	.04472	.04039	.03650	.03302
14.	.12520	.11102	.09855	.08757	.07789	.06934	.06180	.05512	.04921	.04398	.03934	.03522	.03155	.02830	.02540
15.	.10793	.09489	.08352	.07359	.06491	.05731	.05065	.04481	.03969	.03518	.03122	.02773	.02465	.02194	.00195
16.	.09304	.08110	.07078	.06184	.05409	.04736	.04152	.03643	.03201	.02815	.02478	.02183	.01926	.01700	.01503
17.	.08021	.06932	.05998	.05196	.04507	.03914	.03403	.02962	.02581	.02252	.01967	.01719	.01505	.01318	.01156
18.	.06914	.05925	.05083	.04367	.03756	.03235	.02789	.02408	.02082	.01801	.01561	.01354	.01175	.01022	.00889
19.	.05961	.05064	.04308	.03669	.03130	.02673	.02286	.01958	.01679	.01441	.01239	.01066	.00918	.00792	.00684
20.	.05139	.04328	.03651	.03084	.02608	.02209	.01874	.01592	.01354	.01153	.00983	.00839	.00717	.00614	.00526
21.	.04430	.03699	.03094	.02591	.02174	.01826	.01536	.01294	.01092	.00922	.00780	.00661	.00561	.00476	.00405
22.	.03819	.03162	.02622	.02178	.01811	.01519	.01259	.01052	.00880	.00738	.00619	.00520	.00438	.00369	.00311
23.	.03292	.02702	.02222	.01830	.01509	.01247	.01032	.00855	.00710	.00590	.00491	.00410	.00342	.00286	.00184
24.	.02838	.02310	.01883	.01538	.01258	.01031	.00846	.00695	.00573	.00472	.00390	.00323	.00267	.00222	.00184
25.	.02447	.01974	.01596	.01292	.01048	.00852	.00693	.00565	.00462	.00378	.00310	.00254	.00209	.00172	.00142

Exhibit 64

PRESENT VALUE OF $1 PER YEAR

FOR Y YEARS

AT ANNUAL INTEREST RATES OF 1% TO 13%

Year	1%	2%	3%	4%	5%	6%	7%	8%	9%	10%	11%	12%	13%
1.	.9901	.9804	.9709	.9615	.9524	.9434	.9346	.9259	.9174	.9091	.9009	.8929	.8850
2.	1.9704	1.9416	1.9135	1.8861	1.8594	1.8334	1.8080	1.7833	1.7591	1.7355	1.7125	1.6901	1.6681
3.	2.9410	2.8839	2.8286	2.7751	2.7232	2.6730	2.6243	2.5771	2.5313	2.4868	2.4437	2.4018	2.3612
4.	3.9020	3.8077	3.7171	3.6299	3.5459	3.4651	3.3872	3.3121	3.2397	3.1699	3.1024	3.0373	2.9745
5.	4.8535	4.7134	4.5797	4.4518	4.3295	4.2123	4.1002	3.9927	3.8896	3.7908	3.6959	3.6048	3.5172
6.	5.7955	5.6014	5.4172	5.2421	5.0757	4.9173	4.7665	4.6229	4.4859	4.3553	4.2305	4.1114	3.9976
7.	6.7282	6.4720	6.2302	6.0020	5.7863	5.5824	5.3893	5.2064	5.0329	4.8684	4.7122	4.5638	4.4226
8.	7.6517	7.3254	7.0196	6.7327	6.4632	6.2098	5.9713	5.7466	5.5348	5.3349	5.1461	4.9676	4.7988
9.	8.5661	8.1622	7.7861	7.4353	7.1078	6.8017	6.5152	6.2469	5.9852	5.7590	5.5370	5.3282	5.1317
10.	9.4714	8.9825	8.5302	8.1109	7.7217	7.3601	7.0236	6.7101	6.4176	6.1446	5.8892	5.6502	5.4262
11.	10.3677	9.7868	9.2526	8.7604	8.3064	7.8868	7.4987	7.1389	6.8052	6.4951	6.2055	5.9377	5.6869
12.	11.2552	10.5733	9.9539	9.3850	8.8632	8.3838	7.9427	7.5361	7.1607	6.8137	6.4924	6.1944	5.9176
13.	12.1338	11.3483	10.6349	9.9856	9.3935	8.8527	8.3576	7.9038	7.4869	7.1034	6.7499	6.4235	6.1218
14.	13.0038	12.1062	11.2960	10.5631	9.8986	9.2950	8.7454	8.2442	7.7861	7.3677	6.9819	6.6282	6.3025
15.	13.8651	12.8492	11.9379	11.1183	10.3796	9.7122	9.1079	8.5595	8.0607	7.6061	7.1919	6.8109	6.4624
16.	14.7180	13.5777	12.5610	11.6522	10.8377	10.1059	9.4466	8.8514	8.3125	7.8237	7.3792	6.9740	6.6039
17.	15.5624	14.2918	13.1660	12.1656	11.2740	10.4772	9.7632	9.1216	8.5436	8.0215	7.5488	7.1196	6.7291
18.	16.3984	14.9920	13.7534	12.6592	11.6895	10.8276	10.0591	9.3719	8.7556	8.2014	7.7016	7.2497	6.8399
19.	17.2261	15.6784	14.3237	13.1339	12.0853	11.1581	10.3356	9.6036	8.9501	8.3649	7.8393	7.3658	6.9380
20.	18.0547	16.3514	14.8774	13.5903	12.4622	11.4699	10.5940	9.8181	9.1285	8.5136	7.9633	7.4694	7.0248
21.	18.8571	17.0111	15.4149	14.0291	12.8211	11.7640	10.8355	10.0168	9.2922	8.6487	8.0751	7.5620	7.1016
22.	19.6605	17.6580	15.9368	14.4511	13.1630	12.0416	11.0612	10.2007	9.4424	8.7715	8.1757	7.6466	7.1695
23.	20.4559	18.2921	16.4435	14.8568	13.4485	12.3033	11.2722	10.3710	9.5802	8.8832	8.2664	7.7184	7.2297
24.	21.2435	18.9139	16.9355	15.2469	13.7986	12.5503	11.4693	10.5287	9.7066	8.9847	8.3481	7.7843	7.2829
25.	22.0233	19.5234	17.4131	15.6220	14.0939	12.7833	11.6536	10.6748	9.8226	9.0770	8.4217	7.8431	7.3300

Exhibit 65

PRESENT VALUE OF $1 PER YEAR

FOR Y YEARS

AT ANNUAL INTEREST RATES OF 14% TO 26%

Year	14%	15%	16%	17%	18%	19%	20%	21%	22%	23%	24%	25%	26%
1.	.8772	.8696	.8621	.8547	.8475	.8403	.8333	.8264	.8197	.8130	.8065	.8000	.7937
2.	1.6467	1.6257	1.6052	1.5852	1.5656	1.5465	1.5278	1.5095	1.4915	1.4740	1.4568	1.4400	1.4235
3.	2.3216	2.2832	2.2459	2.2096	2.1743	2.1399	2.1065	2.0739	2.0422	2.0114	1.9813	1.9520	1.9234
4.	2.9137	2.8550	2.7982	2.7432	2.6901	2.6386	2.5887	2.5404	2.4936	2.4483	2.4043	2.3616	2.3202
5.	3.4331	3.3522	3.2743	3.1993	3.1272	3.0576	2.9906	2.9260	2.8636	2.8035	2.7454	2.6893	2.6351
6.	3.8887	3.7845	3.6847	3.5892	3.4976	3.4098	3.3255	3.2446	3.1669	3.0923	3.0205	2.9514	2.8850
7.	4.2883	4.1604	4.0386	3.9224	3.8115	3.7057	3.6046	3.5079	3.4155	3.3270	3.2423	3.1611	3.0833
8.	4.6389	4.4873	4.3436	4.2072	4.0776	3.9544	3.8372	3.7256	3.6193	3.5179	3.4212	3.3289	3.2407
9.	4.9464	4.7716	4.6065	4.4506	4.3030	4.1633	4.0310	3.9054	3.7863	3.6731	3.5655	3.4631	3.3657
10.	5.2161	5.0188	4.8332	4.6586	4.4941	4.3389	4.1925	4.0541	3.9232	3.7993	3.6819	3.5715	3.4648
11.	5.4527	5.2337	5.0286	4.8364	4.6560	4.4865	4.3271	4.1769	4.0354	3.9018	3.7757	3.6564	3.5435
12.	5.6603	5.4206	5.1971	4.9884	4.7932	4.6105	4.4392	4.2785	4.1274	3.9852	3.8514	3.7251	3.6060
13.	5.8424	5.5831	5.3423	5.1183	4.9095	4.7147	4.5327	4.3624	4.2028	4.0530	3.9124	3.7801	3.6555
14.	6.0021	5.7245	5.4675	5.2293	5.0081	4.8023	4.6106	4.4317	4.2646	4.1082	3.9616	3.8241	3.6949
15.	6.1422	5.8474	5.5755	5.3242	5.0916	4.8759	4.6755	4.4890	4.3152	4.1530	4.0013	3.8593	3.7261
16.	6.2651	5.9542	5.6685	5.4053	5.1624	4.9377	4.7296	4.5364	4.3567	4.1894	4.0333	3.8874	3.7509
17.	6.3729	6.0472	5.7487	5.4746	5.2226	4.9897	4.7746	4.5755	4.3908	4.2190	4.0591	3.9099	3.7705
18.	6.4674	6.1280	5.8178	5.5339	5.2732	5.0333	4.8122	4.6079	4.4187	4.2431	4.0799	3.9279	3.7861
19.	6.5504	6.1982	5.8775	5.5845	5.3162	5.0700	4.8435	4.6346	4.4415	4.2627	4.0967	3.9424	3.7985
20.	6.6231	6.2593	5.9288	5.6278	5.3527	5.1009	4.8696	4.6567	4.4603	4.2786	4.1103	3.9539	3.8083
21.	6.6870	6.3125	5.9731	5.6648	5.3837	5.1268	4.8913	4.6750	4.4756	4.2916	4.1212	3.9631	3.8161
22.	6.7429	6.3587	6.0113	5.6964	5.4099	5.1486	4.9094	4.6900	4.4882	4.3021	4.1300	3.9705	3.8223
23.	6.7921	6.3988	6.0442	5.7234	5.4321	5.1668	4.9245	4.7025	4.4985	4.3106	4.1371	3.9764	3.8273
24.	6.8351	6.4338	6.0726	5.7465	5.4509	5.1822	4.9371	4.7128	4.5070	4.3176	4.1428	3.9811	3.8312
25.	6.8729	6.4641	6.0971	5.7662	5.4669	5.1951	4.9476	4.7213	4.5139	4.3232	4.1474	3.9849	3.8342

Index